ADVANCE PRAISE

"Great look at how to find the right franchise for you (perfectly named book)! Chapter 3 is worth the price of the book all by itself. It lays out a great process to go from where you are now to finding that right franchise. Excellent!"

-Dave ____ Founder, Mahana Fresh,
____th USA & Firenza Pizza

"D____ ____ ____ ____ ____ ____ ____ rceived safety as an employee of a company or take the plunge into self-employment involves a great deal of introspection and thoughtful analysis. This decision may be one of the most important decisions someone makes in their lives and for many people it's difficult to know where to begin and what questions to ask. This book begins where everyone who starts this journey should begin...what kind of life do I want to live and am I ready to be a business owner?

The Right Franchise For You provides the vital information necessary to help you make an informed decision about buying a franchise. The book covers everything you need to know, such as questions to ask yourself to determine what type of franchise is right for you, what to look for in a Franchise Disclosure Document, the Discovery Day process, what options are available to fund your franchise, how to conduct your due-diligence and much more.

If you are thinking of buying a franchise, you owe it to yourself to buy this book and use it as a guide to help you navigate the often-confusing process of franchise ownership."

-Dallas Kerley, CEO, Benetrends Financial

"Both entertaining and informative, *The Right Franchise For You* pulls back the curtain on franchising and introduces a world of opportunity we rarely hear about. Relatable stories and easy-to-follow steps make it easy to believe that the dream of escaping the 9-5, generating wealth and living life on your own terms really can come true for almost anyone. A great place to start for anyone thinking of starting their own business!"

-Susan Schwartz, CEO, You Who Branding

"This is a book from someone who has walked the walk and helped hundreds of people understand franchising. Faizun has done an amazing job laying out a roadmap into the heart of franchise ownership. If you are looking to achieve the American Dream of business ownership, this is a must read!"

-Nick Neonakis, CEO,
The Franchise Consulting Company

"Kamal is an excellent storyteller. She created an informative and entertaining read for anyone seeking franchise opportunities."

-Jill Abrahamsen, Editor In Chief,
Franchise Dictionary Magazine

"Relatable and insightful, "The Right Franchise for You" is a must-read for anyone considering franchise opportunities. With personal anecdotes, Kamal effectively blends the "how-to" of franchise investigation with the deeper motivation or "why" of everyone's journey toward franchise ownership."

-Ben Reist, Franchise Development
Director, Moran Family of Brands

"Faizun Kamal has masterfully demystified the process of becoming a successful franchise owner. Through her fluid storytelling, with real world examples from her work experience, she makes the process come alive. Her 6 step process of finding the right franchise provides the explorer a road map, with suggested stop overs, to make the leap from a traditional 9 to 5 job, to one of franchise owner. I think the emphasis on self-exploration is critical to moving on this path. Faizun carefully emphasizes the need to understand yourself and your goals, before identifying a possible franchise. The book also describes the value of engaging a franchise coach, who is a valuable partner in the franchise process. I strongly suggest this as the first book a prospective franchise owner should read."

-Bruce Batten, Director, Human Resources,
General Dynamics Mission Systems

"This book is perfect for those that may have experienced frustration with work or where their life is. It seems as if we are often thrust into our careers without doing our own personal "due diligence." I've been laid off just like Sophia's friend, and I know how frustrating and devastating it can be to not know where your next paycheck is going to come from. It can feel hopeless. This is why it's great that Faizun wrote this book to help people know that there are options like franchising out there and there are so many more franchise businesses that we may not be aware of. What I truly appreciate about this book is that it makes it a simple, yet, thorough process that is focused on the individual to find THEIR "perfect fit franchise." I think it's only when we go through a process like that which is outlined in this book that it ultimately leads to more peace, happiness, and fulfillment."

-Gresham Harkless, Founder, Blue16 Media
& Podcast Host, CEO Podcasts

"If you're wondering whether it's time for a change in your life, this book is a must read! It's filled with insights and important information about the journey to business ownership. Let Faizun's experience and wisdom be your guide to understanding how to harness the power of franchising."

-Sherri Seiber, Chief Operating Officer, FranFund

"I first met Faizun Kamal at an event. Since then I have reached out to her on many occasions for advice on business and finance. Finding the strength to pursue your dreams is never easy, many times you don't know where to begin. Faizun Kamal has provided not just encouragement like most others, but a plan on how to achieve the unthinkable. From sharing her own personal journey to helping you plot out your own, this book takes the guess work out of how to be your own boss. What sets The Right Franchise for You apart is that it's not network marketing. This book talks about how to make real business decisions from startup finance, due diligence to mitigate risk, creating business models and more! I cannot think of a better mentor to speak on the topic of franchise opportunities than Faizun."

-Wayne M Dolese Jr, Employment/Pre-Investment Background Screening Professional

"As Thomas Edison once said: "Our greatest weakness lies in giving up." Faizun Kamal is brilliant! Her wisdom that one's comfort zone and fear derails dreams is spot on. The ingredients of this book are filled with endless dreams! Don't give up on your recipe of owning your own business!"

-Mona Janes, President,
Creative Funding by Design

"Making a change is never easy! Faizun Kamal nails the complexities, angst and eventual rewards of a detailed path you can follow to find your passion and freedom. Having personally experienced how she works with her clients, I can testify to the trust, respect and gratitude she earns from all."

-Ricki Wilkins, Senior Franchise
Developer, Deka Lash!

"A must read for anyone looking at purchasing a franchise. Faizun takes a process that frequently overwhelms and shows in plain English, how to approach the purchase of a franchise by breaking each step down into easy-to-digest, bite-sized pieces. Well done on the book!"

-Ralph Nilssen, Business Development Officer,
Guidant Financial

"Are you treading water in life? Are you unhappy with your job? Are you fearful of going out on your own in business because you lack the entrepreneurial experience?

All of these are legitimate symptoms that feel part of a larger economic disorder. And, *The Right Franchise for You: Escape the 9 to 5, Generate Wealth, & Live Life on Your Terms* by experienced franchise coach, Faizun Kamal, attempts to be the panacea to what ails you. Using the franchise as a model, Kamal writes in The Right Franchise for You a six-step process for how you can leave mediocrity behind and find a business that fits your goals.

Faizun Kamal brings a stellar, nearly two decade *Fortune 500* professional career and an MBA to her franchise specialist role in helping you choose the right franchise to start. Now, here in 2019, she has culminated her work and educational experience with her franchise coaching expertise to bring you *The Right Franchise for You.*

The book is structured in 11 chapters; chapters three to nine are the substantive chapters that describe and walk you through *The Six-Step Process for Finding the Franchise That Is Right for You.* Kamal uses the first few chapters to outline the right audience for this book, her background and experience, and whether the entrepreneurial life is good for you and your family. She illuminates numerous people that she's worked with, and their experiences of going from unique positions in life to owning successful franchises.

The book was paced well, and it didn't include fluff in the chapters that focused on the six steps. Some poignant aspects of starting a franchise really highlight the value of the book, including her discussion of choosing and being chosen by a franchise (Chapters 6 to 7), financing your franchise (Chapter 8), and working with a franchise coach (Chapter 10). I was surprised at how interesting the explication of the Franchise Disclosure Document (FDD) was (call me a geek), but it was worth the read just to get a glimpse into the importance of all 23 sections of the FDD!

The book ends with an empowering, impassioned dare by Kamal, that if a franchise is right for you, to start the process of finding the right franchise fit for you.

Faizun Kamal sent me a digital galley copy of the book and I was skeptical that I would learn much or be entertained by a book on franchising. Thankfully, I was pleasantly surprised that, having worked in small business development centers for more than a decade, I learned more than a few things about the franchise experience. With confidence and clarity, Kamal succeeds at providing six steps that are practical, practicable, and possible for anyone interested in living the franchise entrepreneur's life."

-Ray Sidney-Smith, W3 Consulting Inc

"Very inspiring read about the author's journey from the corporate world into the franchising world. A good read for anyone considering a similar move. Once I started the book I couldn't put it down. There is an eloquent linguistic gem in there that I particularly liked - "Like a butterfly in chrysalis, I felt an elemental metamorphosis begin inside me."

-Binita Mehta, Senior Developer,
Gannett/ USA Today Network

"The Right Franchise For You will resonate for those that struggle being a hostage or refugee of corporate America! This is a great read for anyone in the corporate world seeking and understanding the possibilities of franchise ownership...It tells a *story* that is real and relevant vs being "another resource" book. A true road map of taking off the "golden handcuffs" of the corporate world and understanding how to open the doors of education and exploration to make the dream of franchise ownership a reality..."

-Michael Ciccarelli, Franchise Consultant,
The Franchise Consulting Company

"In *The Right Franchise For You*, Faizun craftily boiled down her years of experience in franchising into a simple, executable blueprint that should be an essential read for anyone considering franchise ownership. By highlighting first-hand examples of the way franchising has dramatically changed her life, and those of her clients, Faizun details how tangible the entrepreneurial dream can be for people at all stages in their careers. Practical yet inspirational advice that as a franchisor I would highly recommend."

-Jonathan Thiessen, Chief Development Officer, Home Franchise Concepts

"*The Right Franchise for You* is chock full of great insights and advice for someone that is navigating the franchise process. With real world examples, she makes an easy-to-read book that I read in one sitting. It is a resource book that I will keep at hand and use frequently."

-Heidi Morrissey, President, Kitchen Tune-Up

"Faizun Kamal's book takes you on a journey with a writing style you can not only connect with, but one that brings the book to life. I found myself re-living my own life experiences with distinct emotions as Faizun walked me through individual stories and descriptions of client's lives. I love the perspective on the entrepreneur's world. Too often, the business community forgets about the small business owner!"

-Christopher James Conner, CEO, Franchise Marketing Systems

"There is simply a source that exists within us all screaming for us to let it roam free and do the work of the Blessed among us. So these words of the Author are the most fitting words from which to offer a review. I am unable to think of a better way to describe when one finds the truer calling and embarks on bringing freedom to others through Franchise Business ownership. It is a tale that many experience and Faizun masterfully guides those she cares for through this maze of fear and anxiety with elation and joy.

"Walking through the sun-dappled shade, little did I know that my own transformation was about to begin! I was never going back to the corporate world. I was done. There was no two ways about it. I no longer cared for what that lifestyle required. I had done it for almost eight years, and I no longer wanted to return to it. I stopped looking for happiness in the same place I had lost it."

We all need a guide and mentor for those transitional phases of our life. Well done, Faizun!"

-Robert Addie, ActionCOACH

"I have discovered something incredibly impressive: I just read a 176-page book that thoroughly and concisely communicated nearly everything I have learned about the franchise process during my time studying franchising at my fully accredited private university... and then some. So here is my advice to those considering a career in the franchise community: Go to school and pursue a formal education in franchising or read this book. If you proceed without one of the two, you are foregoing a wealth of critical information that will set your business up for success. Kamal is clearly an expert in the field with experiential wisdom to offer. The book is an easy read that brings clarity and practicality to several complicated but important topics. I will be keeping this book nearby for future reference throughout my career in franchising."

-Eva Bracciale, Student

"From the very first few pages, the author brings you into the head and world of most people. Struggling to balance work and home, making money for another who cares nothing about you and onto the inner turmoil of the average American. This gripping book will grab your attention and walk you down the path of making a real life change."

-Julie Kreider, Franchise Consultant, The Franchise Consulting Company

"Upon reading the first few pages of this book, I could instantly relate to Sophia! Having worked as an entrepreneur for most of my life and then merging with a large firm, I became an employee overnight and lost the freedom and flexibility that I was so accustomed to. I started looking around for a side business that would give me the sense of ownership that I so badly missed and started working with a franchise broker. This is the best decision I ever made! They matched me up with a franchise that was directly aligned with my interests and I purchased a franchise in an industry I was so passionate about! I would highly recommend this book if you're looking into transitioning into franchise ownership! Simply life changing!"

-Diane Wilson, Franchise Development Director, Tutor Doctor

"I have been in the franchising industry for nearly 15 years and have read many books on how to research a franchise concept. What makes this book unique, is the way the stories are very relatable to the experiences of my clients. It is a personal relationship that needs to be nurtured between a franchise coach and someone who is looking to be in control of their own life through franchise ownership. It is a scary, but very necessary process. Faizun has done a wonderful job in combining real world experiences with a proven step-by-step process to show how it should be done! This is a very engaging and well thought out book."

-Troy Molen, Franchise Licensing Advisor,
Home Franchise Concepts

"*The Right Franchise for You* is an educational and revealing guide in the quest to obtaining long term security and personal fulfillment through business ownership. Faizun soundly illustrates that there is growing insecurity and dissatisfaction in perceived job security. As an award winning entrepreneur, franchise expert and someone who has helped thousands acquire, fund, sell and exit their business; I would encourage you examine Faizun's expert advice to not only help you avoid costly mistakes but help you discover the best path to finding *The RIGHT franchise for you*".

-Larry Carnell, Vice President of Development,
Benetrends Financial

"Faizun Kamal has filled a gap with this excellent guide. It walks you through the specific steps required to become a franchisee. It shines a light on a process that is easily misunderstood and where it is sometimes hard to find information regarding the process. She provides meaningful real life examples to point out where individuals are faced with potential pitfalls and how one's own choices are key to ultimate success. This book has helped me already."

-Debon Thornton, President, D.R. Resources, Inc

"This book is for career changers, those in career transition, people looking to start their own business, entrepreneurs- and virtually anyone looking to find what's missing in their professional life. "The Right Franchise for you" addresses the 'why' for franchising! It could provide the answer you've been looking for and bridge the gap between being stuck in a job that doesn't fit your needs and a career you'll love! If anyone has ever considered owning their own business and being their own boss, *The Right Franchise for You* could be the answer you've been looking for! Faizun provides a step by step approach and all the tools you need to find the best franchise for YOUR needs. A must read for anyone considering franchise ownership!"

-Dawn Bye, Product Development
Expert in career transition

"As a young professional just starting out, trying to find my place in my chosen career path, I wake up stress dreaming of what was left undone at work far too often. Kamal writes to us coming from a place of understanding the itch to make a difference, to be successful, and to build your brand in your work life. Isn't that what drives us to work so hard, day in and day out? Then, she brings back the reality of the American Dream and how we are supposed to enjoy the little moments, leave work behind on the weekends, and just live freely with our loved ones, with the things that spark joy in us. I personally can't remember the last time I felt that freedom, therefore I seek balance and hope in reading *The Right Franchise For You* knowing that I can have a successful work life and be a fully engaged person in my personal life. I long for the carefree days before the 9-5 lifestyle, and with Kamal's mindfulness reminders, I plan to get back to that happy place."

-Daniella Wade, Digital Content, MainGate Inc

"This book will answer so many questions future franchise/business owners have. An easy and very informative read! I will personally be recommending this book to everyone I know who wants to be a franchise owner. Faizun is simply the best when it comes to this!"

-Nico Garcia Moreyra, Franchisee,
Two Maids & A Mop

"The Right Franchise For You" is a must-read, both for the person planning on buying a franchise and the person selling a franchise. Faizun lays out all the aspects one needs to consider in an easy-to-follow step-by-step approach honing in on such crucial topics as, is it the right fit for you? If you cannot answer yes to this, then don't pass go. She gives clear guidance on navigating all the aspects of franchising from profit margins to legal issues. I highly recommend this book."

-Sitki Kazanci, Founder & Publisher,
Franchise Connect Magazine

"This is a MUST READ for any person who wants to start anything new in life and not just franchising. Faizun has carved out a blueprint that anybody who seriously wants a better life from what he or she is currently going through, can pick and apply to his or her situation and succeed. The book is filled with practical down-to-earth and detailed information that is easy to apply for positive results. It is also very reader-friendly with a freshness and simplicity in presentation that only a person who is walking her talk can deliver.

I love the way the book is beautifully speckled with practical real life experiences, each perfectly timed for the reader to capture exactly how it feels to be in such a situation. I am so proud of my friend Faizun for making franchising a reality for anyone who cares to consider it."

-Abigail Kyei, President, Ghana
College of Nurses and Midwives

"I have read many books on the topic of franchising and this is among the best! Ms. Kamal shares real life stories, including her own, that quickly establishes her understanding of the wants and needs within so many of us who have longed for the freedoms and rewards of business ownership. Her vast personal and professional experiences combine with eloquent words to paint vivid pictures of possibilities and authentic encouragement for anyone who has ever yearned for more. Highly recommend!"

-Eileen Proctor, Director of Franchise Development,
Franchise Fastlane

"As a seasoned franchisor and avid reader, this book nailed it by providing transparency and guidance in a clear and concise manner. Very informative - strongly recommend for those exploring embarking on a new endeavor or reevaluating where you are at in your life by opening up possibilities."

-Angela Olea, CEO, Assisted Living Locators

"This book is written by a woman who definitely knows business. It is very helpful and will help you get to your dreams in no time. I HIGHLY recommend. Mrs. Faizun is a genius..."

-Jermel Richmond, Ordnance Officer,
United States Army

"Faizun is an expert in franchise consulting and has written a book that any prospective franchisee should read. Her advice to validate the franchise is on target - talk to franchisees, read the FDD and retain experienced franchise counsel to advise you. The book is written in an easy, conversational manner which makes it easy reading for everyone. I highly recommend this book."

-Nancy Lanard, Founder, Lanard & Associates

"We fear what we do not understand. And fear prevents many potentially great entrepreneurs from properly exploring the opportunity to go into business for themselves. *The Right Franchise for You* is an invaluable resource for anyone who has considered going into business for themselves. Faizun provides a comprehensive blueprint for how to think about, identify, and evaluate the right franchise."

-David Nilssen, CEO, Guidant Financial

"Having a background in corporate and then later finding franchising, I appreciated the vulnerability and straight forward guidance to the stories and the expectations of the process in investigating franchise concepts that are shared in this book. For anyone questioning, if the "mundane" is the norm, read this and you'll be surprised by your new perspective!"

-Ashly Loza, Director of Brand
Development, Raintree

Foreword by **WILLIAM ROSENZWEIG**
Co-Chair at Berkeley Haas Center for Responsible Business

The RIGHT Franchise for You

escape the 9 to 5, generate wealth,
& live life on your terms

FAIZUN KAMAL

NEW YORK

LONDON • NASHVILLE • MELBOURNE • VANCOUVER

The Right Franchise for You

Escape the 9 to 5, Generate Wealth, & Live Life on your Terms

© 2020 Faizun Kamal

Published in New York, New York, by Morgan James Publishing in partnership with Difference Press. Morgan James is a trademark of Morgan James, LLC. www.MorganJamesPublishing.com

ISBN 9781642798685 paperback
ISBN 9781642798692 eBook
Library of Congress Control Number: 2019952055

Cover Design Concept: Jennifer Stimson

Cover & Interior Design: Chris Treccani   www.3dogcreative.net

Editor: Moriah Howell

Book Coaching: The Author Incubator

Morgan James is a proud partner of Habitat for Humanity Peninsula and Greater Williamsburg. Partners in building since 2006.

Get involved today! Visit
MorganJamesPublishing.com/giving-back

My parents, you're why I wrote this book.
My husband, the love of my life.
My daughter, my North Star.
My sister, the "other" wonder woman.

TABLE OF CONTENTS

FOREWORD

I s it possible to bring your whole self to work every day, so that who you are and what you do are in a state of fulfilling harmony and alignment? And is it possible to do so and create a life of financial security and abundance?

Faizun Kamal thinks so. She's living it, for herself, and as a caring, effective guide for many others.

In the pages that follow, Faizun shares her pathways for nothing short of personal and professional transformation. While this book is focused on finding the right fit toward a franchise opportunity, her stories and guidance have far reaching impact for all aspects of life and work.

In Faizun's insightful words and experience, she shows precisely how it's possible to reinvent oneself. In her own life, she has journeyed from harried corporate executive to independent, fulfilled, entrepreneurial business leader. In the course of her adventure, she comes to better understand how to care for herself, her family and a broader community of fellow seekers. She has escaped the proverbial rat race by realigning her personal values with her work and has found the way toward a kind of personal and professional freedom she only once dreamed about.

She wants to help you do this, too.

The Right Franchise for You is, at once, a candid personal memoir and a valuable guide to professional reinvention. It is filled with moving personal stories, marked by humanness and vulnerability. Faizun is generous with her insightful advice and expertise and brings a sense of honest, joyful effort to everything she chooses to do. You'll enjoy this easy-reading journey with her – as if she was coaching you personally toward your dream of a meaningful livelihood.

I met Faizun as she began to explore moving beyond the perplexing confines of her prestigious corporate job. She (like you might be right now) was bristling at the paradoxes of looking professionally great on the outside, yet feeling unsatisfied, mis-placed, on the inside. There was something complex, deep and important missing for her and she knew she had to do something about it. She started where you might be right now: By studying and searching for guidance from experts.

We first had a chance to speak together at a University symposium on social entrepreneurship. Over the years, I am proud to say I was a mentor who has become a friend: a "friendtor." But now the gifts are all mine to receive, as I am learning much more from Faizun as she pushes ahead to share her bounty of wisdom and experience. She brings a contagious spark of joy and purpose to her guidance and a deep commitment to reciprocity that you will experience as you make your way through this book's chapters.

This effective handbook will certainly fulfill your curiosity and answer your questions about how to find the right franchise opportunity. But my sense is that it will do much more for you. What Faizun shares here is a manual for personal liberation and professional transformation. Her guidance comes from an awakened heart and a wise mind.

Won't you join her on this journey? There's no one I would trust more as a brave and skilled guide toward finding and making the most meaningful work, and life, possible.

Will Rosenzweig
Healdsburg, California
June 2019

Living the American Dream... or Nightmare?

"People are literally dying for a paycheck."
– Jeffrey Pfeffer

Through the distant recesses of her sleep-filled mind, Sophia hears bells tinkling. Insistently. She finally opens her eyes. It's four a.m., and the alarm is blaring. Turning it off, she lies in bed looking up at the ceiling. All is quiet. Jonathan is still asleep and won't be up for another hour or so. Her mind immediately revs up. She starts thinking about the day ahead. What meetings does she have? What deadlines does she have to meet? A lifetime of being in the corporate world had wired her this way. Then she remembers...

It's Sunday. She let's out a small sigh of relief. She has a reprieve for at least one more day before she's back in the of-

1

fice again. As the thought occurs, the familiar deflated feeling pools in the pit of her stomach.

Downstairs, she makes a pot of milk oolong tea. As the water boils and fills the air with the delicate fragrance, Sophia looks out onto the deck. The red cardinal, her very own guardian angel, is sitting on the old oak tree. She smiles involuntarily. She first noticed the little red bird three months ago when Anne, her best friend at work, had gotten laid off. Anne's layoff had impacted her deeply. This wasn't the first time that a colleague and friend had been let go by her employer. She couldn't help but wonder when she would be on the chopping block.

For a moment, Sophia feels paralyzed, panicking. If she gets laid off like Anne, she does not know what she will do. Sipping her steaming, milky tea, a deep sense of exhaustion and emptiness comes over her. Her mind wanders to the situation in her office.

It has been three months since Anne was let go. The company had been going through wave after wave of layoffs. At the office, she hears various euphemisms to describe what is happening: reorganizing, trimming the fat, restructuring. Whatever the term being used, the end result is always the same. Numerous colleagues had left over the past year. When she walks down the hallway at work, she notices more and more dark and empty offices. With her colleagues, she feels that the energy is changed. There is a palpable sense of foreboding and unease among everyone. No one speaks openly about what is happening, but everyone feels the air of uncertainty and thinks about it all the time.

Every Monday, Sophia starts the week with dread wondering if this will be her last week at work. Every Friday, she goes home oddly relieved that she still has a job. While she no longer loves what she does, she is scared of getting laid off. She has been with her company for almost ten years. She is good at what she does; she just does not love it. With each year that goes by, she moves up the proverbial corporate ladder. She makes very good money – money that enables them to live in a sought-after neighborhood, send their two daughters to private schools, and take nice vacations to exotic locales each year.

As the Vice President of Marketing Strategy, she has a fancy title and a corner office. She has a small team that reports to her. And as the saying goes: when you pick up one end of the stick, you pick up the other! While she has these senior management perks, her work also brings with it an ever-increasing list of headaches. With each additional year in the company, Sophia is given more and more responsibilities without the accompanying support or resources. She is overworked and feels under-appreciated. As the company "tightened its belt" and laid off expensive management staff, they also decreased the bonus payouts each year to continue to "stay lean and competitive." So, while her responsibilities have increased, there has not been a corresponding increase in her paycheck. With each year that passes, Sophia feels the weight at work get progressively heavier and heavier.

After her best friend's layoff, these thoughts are ever-present in her mind. She cannot shake off an impending sense of doom, like a ticking time bomb that mocks her as if to say, "You're next in line!"

More than once, Sophia has talked to her husband about leaving her job, but they will lose the health insurance, the company match into her retirement account, the (shrinking) yearly bonus. With the passage of time, the golden handcuffs around her wrists grow ever tighter…

Over the past ten years, she feels that she has constantly had to choose between work and her family. When she first started at the company, she was forty-one years old. She and Jonathan had been married for a few years. A year later, she had Emma. Her pregnancy was tough, fraught with unknowns. Her doctor labeled her "high risk" because of her age. Emma came into this world through an emergency c-section. Sophia spent the next ten days in the hospital. Twenty-seven days after that, she was back at work in her corner office.

As her mind wanders into the past, her eyes tear up. To date, the biggest regret of her life is that she has almost completely missed the first year of Emma's life. Other than a few home videos and pictures that she and her husband had taken, she doesn't really have a lot of memories of Emma's first year of life. At fifty-one days old, Emma started daycare. Sophia dropped her off before dawn to head straight to work and picked her up around seven p.m. before returning home. She barely spent any time with her daughter during her waking hours. Looking back at the time, she remembers how she wondered if her daughter even knew who her mother was.

As Sophia entered into an ever-increasing cycle of stress at work with impossible deadlines and multiple bosses with conflicting agendas, she had her second daughter, Isabelle. She tried to be more present in her life, but always felt that she never quite hit the mark with either of them.

As the years went on, Sophia continued to miss milestone events with both of her daughters: Emma's first basketball game, Isabelle's school performance at Thanksgiving, and so many others that she has now lost track of… or has she just put it out of her mind to assuage the guilt? The guilt is a dull, dead weight that feels like a hard stone in her chest.

In moments of brutal honesty, she feels that her job has become the proverbial "albatross around her neck." She needs it to pay the mortgage and all the bills, yet she also feels her soul dying a little bit every single day. Once again the panic rises up like a wave inside her. She feels trapped, her back up against the wall. She has given this job everything but knows that she is just a number on the company's balance sheet. When the day comes that they deem her "too expensive" to keep around, she too will be let go, just like Anne and all the others before her.

As dawn breaks and wisps of pink light up the morning sky, Sophia starts to cry silently. This job has not just robbed her of precious family moments that she will never get back; it has also robbed her of her health. Four years into her job, she is diagnosed with high blood pressure and diabetes. At every health checkup, her doctor advises her to reduce her stress. "Take a yoga class," says her doctor. She silently nods her head, knowing exactly what she needs to do to reduce her stress – and it isn't yoga! "It's ironic," she thinks. "The job I have held on to in order to continue to have health insurance for myself and my family is the same job that has stolen my health from me!"

Sipping her tea, she dries her cheeks and looks out over the deck. Cocking its little head, the red cardinal looks intently back at her before flying off. Putting down her cup, she sits up straight, something welling up inside her. "I will not continue to live my life like this. Not anymore. I need more, want more. There must be something else I can do! I'm well-educated, have managed large teams, and solve problems everyday! I cannot stomach the thought of another eight years with the company, assuming of course that they don't lay me off first! I need more flexibility in my life so I can finally be with my girls and sit down to dinner with my husband without checking my phone fifteen times. I want to make as much money as I now do and more... What can I do?"

Questions swirl in Sophia's head, and then she remembers. After getting laid off, her friend Anne had attended an event for job seekers and professionals in career transition. The keynote speaker was a franchise expert, a woman who had talked passionately about her own experiences as a corporate executive. After getting laid off by her employer, the franchise expert talked about being a corporate refugee and searching for a career option that allowed her all the things she had craved for years but had not been able to achieve in the corporate world: financial freedom, time flexibility, work/life balance, personal fulfilment. She had finally found her ideal career and life when she found the world of franchises.

Franchises!?

After the workshop, Anne had gone up to talk to the speaker because her story had resonated so intimately with hers. When Anne told Sophia about the conversation, she heard the excitement in Anne's voice. She had not heard that in the years that they had worked together. Anne had already set up an appointment with her. "I think I will do the same! I want to find out more about if a franchise makes sense for me and my family!" thought Sophia excitedly.

As she makes up her mind to speak with the franchise expert, more questions pop into her mind. "What franchise is right for me? What skills do I need as a franchisee? Will my skillset be a fit? How much money can I make? What if it doesn't work out? Will I have to work at it full-time and for how many years? Will I have any flexibility at all? How will I know that the franchise I choose is the right one for me?"

Opening her laptop, she googles "franchises for corporate executives" and the franchise expert's name. Up pops the search results and the speaker's book on the very topic of how to find the right franchise! As she reads the book description, Sophia's excitement grows. The book talks about exactly the questions she has in her mind!

Sophia hits the purchase button. While waiting to receive the book in the mail, she has access to the first chapter online and begins reading. Who is this author, this woman, who seems to know her journey and her pain so intimately? It is almost as though the book is written just for her.

Why Franchising Made Sense (for Sophia and Anne)

As you may have guessed by now, Sophia was a client of mine. As she tells her story, she found me through her best friend, Anne, another client. Both Sophia and Anne are now franchisees in two of the most reputable and well-known franchise brands in the country. Their lives now, compared to when they were corporate executives, could not be any more different.

As professional women, they spent decades of their lives dedicated to producing the best work for their employers. In the process, they sacrificed much. When the pain of the status quo became too great, they finally made the decision to define success on their own terms, achieved it by their own rules and built full lives that they are now proud to live. As franchise business owners, they have the control over their lives that they were missing as employees.

Climbing the corporate ladder is always hard, but it is especially tricky for women. Often, they are considered unambitious compared to male peers, because though they work, they are still the primary care-takers of their families. Some may have to leave the office at 5pm to pick up children from daycare, others cannot attend 7pm meetings because they don't have child-care. Many cannot break away from home for overnight work trips. And for women who took time off to raise their kids, it becomes even more challenging to get back in the workforce. All of these realities chop away at a woman's opportunity for success in the corporate world.

This is why so many ambitious women are opting out of Corporate America and choosing to go the franchise route. Investing in a franchise becomes a very effective, and ultimately very fulfilling way to brave the workforce–but this time, on their own terms and not their employer's.

Owning a franchise is a great option for women who want to work and earn income, but cannot put in the hours that traditional corporate jobs demand. Business ownership gives women the flexibility to grow at their own pace, while working hours that fit with their personal responsibilities.

So, if you are a professional woman who is exhausted of struggling through a corporate career and wants a job that offers lucrative incomes and work-life balance, there may be a franchise out there for you!

Every female client of mine cited flexibility as one of their top reasons for considering a franchise. Having been employees all their lives and intimately understanding the limitations of working for someone else, they were eager to finally find work that they truly had control over. By becoming their own boss, many women feel that they become more productive professionally and more fulfilled personally in their family lives.

Into the Looking Glass

I shared Sophia's story with you because it is the story of so many others! In our country, I believe we are in the midst of a huge silent social epidemic. Thousands of well-qualified and well-educated professionals, both women and men, feel disenfranchised in their careers and their jobs. They feel like they are living life at half measure. There is little to no joy in their professional lives. Their job is not a fit with what they are good at. Every day at the office is soul-crushing. They desperately want to do something different, something that "fits" who they are. They feel stuck because they don't know what "it" is or where to begin to find it.

As you read about Sophia, does something stir inside you? Does it bring up similar feelings that you have had for years that you have pushed aside? Can you almost feel the unwanted weight of your frustrations buried beneath your everyday thoughts? Had you suspected that unpacking your frustrations could change your life and the lives of others? If you have picked up this book and have read this far, then I suspect your answer is a resounding "Yes!"

Did you find parallels of your own life in Sophia's story? If so, read on.

My own story is very similar to Sophia's and, maybe, yours as well.

2

Coloring Outside the Lines

"Everyone has oceans to fly, if they have the heart to do it. Is it reckless? Maybe. But what do dreams know of boundaries?"
– Amelia Earhart

Charting an Unconventional Path

"You have to be odd to be number one," said Dr Seuss. For the majority of my life, I was always the "odd one" out but never felt like number one.

In 1980, growing up in Nigeria as an expat, I stuck out like a sore thumb. In a school of hundreds, I was the only kid with straight hair and Asian features. Years later, in a Bangladesh high school filled with popular kids, I wasn't particularly cool. This trend of never really "fitting in" would continue through the years.

After graduating with a dual degree in women's studies and environmental studies from college, I began working at the World Bank in Bangladesh. As one of the youngest bank employees, I traveled around the region, meeting with villagers to assess the efficacy of bank-funded projects. From there, I then went on to work with the Swiss and Canadian Development Agencies for a couple more years. I liked the work, but again, it felt like I was "out of place." As I progressed through my career, I would create additional responsibilities that were not in my job description. In every job I held, I seemed to always be looking for something more.

For the next decade, I would continue to "color outside the lines" and create an unconventional career path as I searched for my calling.

After graduating with a Master's degree in Public Policy from Johns Hopkins University, I began working for an international development organization. It was work with heart providing people in developing countries with resources to improve their lives. I spent several years there implementing the organization's eighteen-month strategic planning process between headquarters (U.S.) and its three regional offices (India, Guatemala, Burkina Faso). While I enjoyed the work and learned new skills, I continued to wonder whether this was my path.

After a few years there, I went on to work for another non-profit organization that provided healthcare training in developing countries. I spent the next five years there establishing and managing a $22 million country portfolio across Asia, Africa, and Eastern Europe. I traveled extensively, hiring and building teams, and setting up program offices across these regions.

While working there, I had slowly started to get an inkling of where my true passion might lie. I realized that I was fascinated by business, how companies began and grew, and how they impacted the world. While working fulltime, I decided to go back again to graduate school, this time to get a master's in business administration.

As I was finishing up my MBA, I was discovered by a Fortune 15 company. Following a long two-year courtship during which they kept offering me a place on their public policy team, I finally accepted their offer and came on board. I was starting to feel burnt out with all the travel of the past five years and felt that a job that did not require constant travel would be a welcome respite. By this point, I also sensed that the business world was beckoning to me and I had to answer the call.

From a global nomad to a corporate executive, I found myself living the fabled American Dream. Working in corporate America, I got a fancy title with the attendant bells and whistles. I attended prestigious conferences and industry events. I established national programs with numerous organizations and played an active role in shaping the company's public policy agenda. It all sounded very important. Yet, I still felt like the old me and carried around the sense that this, once again, was not my path. I was still the odd one out. And no, it wasn't the imposter syndrome that has recently become very popular in business parlance that I was suffering from. It was something deeper, more intrinsic. My external world did not align with my internal purpose, and I felt conflicted. It was as though my life did not fit me.

While in the corporate world, and armed with an MBA, I started my first company: sourceFK. This was a social enterprise that partnered with women artisans in my native Bangladesh to create markets for their goods in the U.S. As has often happened with big turning points in my life, I met someone who unbeknownst to me at the time, would go on to become a dear mentor and inspire me to come into my own as an entrepreneur. As I was representing my fledgling company at one of the biggest fashion events in New York, I met famed American designer Tory Burch. She was intrigued by how I had built the company and created sustainable livelihoods for hundreds of women who otherwise would have languished in poverty. Impressed by how much we had achieved in such a short time, she wanted to feature my company on the Tory Burch Foundation website. I still smile when I think about that moment. I felt like I was in a dream!

The feature kicked off what would go on to become a long relationship with Tory and her foundation. I was subsequently selected as a Foundation Fellow and named by the Foundation as "A Woman to Watch" – a huge honor that brought with it more publicity and more opportunities. Looking back, I now realize that these opportunities helped to sharpen the saw of my business acumen. I was mentored by founders of well-known companies, and supported with resources to grow my own. When I look back on this time of my life, the most valuable part of this experience was the lesson I learnt from Tory in what it meant to be a role model. As one of the youngest self-made female billionaires, she had charted a fearless path for what is possible. She made no apologies for her ambition and lifted other women as she went along. As I balanced the corporate world with the world of entrepreneurship, what I had been seeking all these years slowly started to come into focus.

Could entrepreneurship be my calling?

Is this what I had been looking for all my life?

At the same time that I was growing my business, sourceFK, I was working a full-time corporate job. I began traveling for work and things only got busier. Then, in 2013, I had my daughter. Motherhood brought me immense joy. It also brought with it "first time parent" challenges and long sleepless nights. Juggling my personal and professional lives started to feel very enervating.

Becoming Businessworthy

As sourceFK grew its retail footprint in the US and abroad, I got busier in my job. The telecom landscape was shifting under our feet and the company was working over-time to maintain its global leadership position. Pressure at work intensified. Then the layoffs began. In the midst of all this, with a seven month old baby, I was accepted into Stanford University's prestigious Social Entrepreneurship Program. This was yet another dream come true! Up until that point, I had grown sourceFK organically. I now wanted a more systematic framework for the next phase of the company's growth.

While at Stanford, I met a gentleman who would go on to become a friend, a mentor and a guide: William Rosenzweig. Will is a businessman with the soul of a poet and the wisdom of a gardener. He is best known for creating the premium tea category as we now know it through his first company, The Republic of Tea. His journey of how he built and grew the company is like none other that I know of. When I met him, I was immediately drawn to his palpable sense of calm and wisdom. After I left Stanford, we continued to stay in touch.

I was excited by the immense potential of a business and the power it had to shape the world for good. I focused on growing sourceFK, my company, by strengthening the local infrastructure of the team in Bangladesh. I continued to bring on additional weaver partners and expanding the scope of our reach. We went on to create numerous partnerships with Tory Burch, Fashion for Development, and other retailers. I started to get invitations to speak about how I had built the company. The oldest speaker agency in the country reached out to me to offer an exclusive speaker's contract. Fashion industry icons like the Fashion Institute of Technology (FIT) and others brought me on as a speaker at their conferences to share the incredible story of our growth and how we were transforming lives of women a world away. We were widely featured in prominent new and traditional media including the Huffington Post, among others.

Over the years, I have learnt much from Will about what it means to be businessworthy – ethically creating economic value that also creates value for society. Will went on to start Physic Ventures, a venture capital firm focusing on funding food businesses. For his groundbreaking work, he received the Oslo Business for Peace Award. This is an award given to an exceptional individual who is selected by an independent committee of Nobel Prize laureates for being businessworthy – ethically and responsibly running a business for the greater good of society.

Doing well by doing good. This has remained my motto and embodies the essence of the work I now do as an entrepreneur and franchise coach.

Life Always Bursts the Boundaries of Formulas

Fast forward to a sunny April day in 2015. The day began like any other. Unbeknownst to me, however, that day would mark the beginning of a journey into a grand adventure: the path towards my calling. All these years of searching for my purpose would finally collide in the most unexpected way.

I had spent that morning in back to back meetings. By noon, my stomach was grumbling. Picking up a sandwich and a cup of tea from Au Bon Pain, I walked back through the park that was right across from the office. Walking through the sun-dappled shade, my mind began to wander. This had been my routine for almost eight years now. With each year that passed, I felt more and more like a shadow. It was as though I was on autopilot, going through the motions of work and life.

Not for the first time, I felt a deep and heavy sadness in my chest. I had always felt that I had so much to offer, yet I was playing small because I was playing someone else's game. We each come into this world with strange and beautiful jewels buried deep inside us. If we are authentic with ourselves, we begin to uncover them. As we put them to use, we begin to live our best fullest lives. We transform our own lives and, in doing so, inspire countless others to do the same!

Walking through the sun-dappled shade, little did I know that my own transformation was about to begin!

Around two p.m., I got a call from my boss asking me to come to his office. Call it my intuition or maybe it was the slight hesitation in his voice, but even before I had hung up the phone, I knew exactly what the conversation was going to be about. I would have to be blind to not read the writing on the wall over the past year. So many of my colleagues had been laid off. They had simply become too expensive for the company to keep on the payroll and so they had been let go.

John ushered me to sit down. I could sense the discomfort he was feeling. Without a lot of preamble, he said that in this most recent round of layoffs, my position had been eliminated. He expressed his apologies and said some other things which I don't remember because I was overwhelmed when I heard that I was being let go. No, not overwhelmed with shock, as you might think, but with an odd combination of elation and relief. Without thinking, I got up and gave him a hug. I am certain that this was the first and the last time that he got a hug for giving someone a pink slip! John and I had always had a great relationship, and he knew that I had been unhappy for quite some time.

I will never forget what I felt as I walked back to my office. It was as though the big boulder that had been pressing down on my chest for the past eight years had finally been lifted off, and I could breathe once more. The relief was enormous. For me, this was a blessing, straight up – not in disguise!

Setting Out on the Path Less Traveled

The next twelve months would prove to be a journey into self-discovery like nothing else I had ever experienced. While I did not know what my destination looked like, the path unfolded with each step I took.

At the time, technology behemoths like Google, Facebook, Uber, and Lyft were all opening up policy offices in Washington D.C. I knew it was only a matter of time before I would be back in an industry that I knew like the back of my hand. I proceeded to do what everyone in career transition does. I immediately jumped into a job search. I spruced up my resume and customized cover letters for different positions. I started reaching out to my professional network on LinkedIn to let them know that I was in transition and to keep me in mind should any opportunity open up. I scheduled informational interviews with friends of friends. Getting a new job was priority number one.

As the interviews started flowing in, and I had quite a few, I started to notice something very curious. By the time I would get to the second or third round of interviews, I would intentionally do something that was contrary to everything that was logical. I remember one particular phone interview. I was speaking with the individual who would be my direct supervisor if I got hired. He asked me what I thought about work-life balance in an industry that was notorious for being fast-paced and stress-ridden. I replied that I thought the industry was unhealthy, that these were unrealistic standards and expectations, that in order to be truly successful every professional should have time to take care of work matters as well as family life. Even as I responded to his question, I knew in my heart that this would be the last time I would be speaking with this particular company. I did not give him the well-worn, tired response that every job seeker would have given and that he had expected: "I will do what is needed to get the job done." In fact, that turned out to be the last call not just with that particular company but the last job-search call I was ever going to make.

Two months into my transition, I came to a conclusion that – in retrospect – was inevitable. I was never going back to the corporate world. I was done. There was no two ways about it. I no longer cared for what that lifestyle required. I had done it for almost eight years, and I no longer wanted to return to it. I finally stopped looking for happiness in the same place I had lost it.

So, while this was a life-changing realization for me, the bigger question still loomed in the background: what was I going to do now?

The next few months that ensued is a time in my life that I refer to as my "dark night of the soul." I don't use this phrase to say that everything was onerous and difficult. I use this phrase to describe a period of deep introspective reflection. Like a butterfly in chrysalis, I felt an elemental metamorphosis begin inside me. It was a time during which I forced myself to ask the hard questions, to be brutally honest with myself about what I wanted, and to clarify my "why."

I know you're thinking: what is she doing? Here I was without a job and income, and instead of lining up another gig, I was getting all philosophical with myself. Well, to give you some context, allow me to tell you a little bit about what my life was like before I got laid off.

You Weren't Born to Just Pay Bills and Die

A simple way to describe my life during my time in the corporate world was this: it was out of whack. I was the living, breathing negative stereotype of the corporate executive. I worked ten-hour days and felt as though my life was moving at a hundred miles an hour. I was always stressed-out, in an industry where the norm was to "break things fast" and keep moving, always moving. My lifestyle had become unhealthy. I barely worked out, and the vending machine in the lunchroom dictated what went into my body. My meals frequently consisted of two or three unhealthy snacks, eaten hunched up over my computer. Our daughter who was around eighteen months at the time was like a stranger to me. I barely saw her or my husband.

I want to be clear that it was not all bad in the corporate world. Nothing is ever all good or bad. As a corporate executive, I did well financially. For that, I will always be grateful because it allowed me to do so much for my family. I made lasting friendships with amazing colleagues. I was mentored by pioneers and giants in the industry. As challenging as it was, this time in my life was deeply formative in teaching me about business. As a business owner now, I am appreciative of the lessons I learned firsthand that people only read about in case studies at business schools. I will always be proud to have been a part of an American business icon that has transformed the technology landscape of this country for millions of people. To this day, I get a little nostalgic when I see ads for the company on TV.

One of the biggest lessons from my corporate days is that money cannot come at the cost of joy. In a society that bombards us with the message that money is the end-all, be-all for ultimate happiness, I found out that this was simply not true for me. While we all need money to live and help out others, it is not the only thing that matters. Not by a long shot. For most of my time in the corporate world, I felt miserable. I was not miserable because the company was bad. I was not miserable because I had a horrible boss. I was miserable because I was a "mis" fit with the work. I was good at my job, but I did not have a passion for it. While many will say that as long as they get a paycheck they are okay with doing whatever the job requires, that too was never true for me. Because I felt I needed the income to provide for my family, I had traded my joy for money. I would not make that mistake ever again.

Stop Making a Living. Start Designing a Life.

The legendary designer Coco Chanel said, "My life didn't please me so I created my life." As a woman who trailblazed the fashion industry, breaking norms and creating new ones, Chanel set out to intentionally redesign her career and life. To this day, her inimitable brand has endured the test of time and remains at the leading edge of a ruthless industry where trends come and go in a heartbeat.

After I had eliminated corporate jobs and working for someone else as viable options, I too knew the time had come to hit the reset button on my career and life. For so long, I had filled my life with activities and things I did not care for. It was time to detox. It was time to shed the dead leaves, so to speak, to allow space for new growth. It was time to re-create and re-design my life.

The months that followed became one of the most personally satisfying and formative time of my life! That summer, I started a home garden. As the tomatoes, cucumbers, and chili peppers grew, my wilted spirit slowly rejuvenated. Running my fingers over the silky skin of the purple eggplants gave me a feeling that I can only describe as pure joy. Kneeling on the ground with the hot sun beating down on my face and the warm moist soil running through my fingers, I felt a groundedness and a peace that I had not felt in a very long time. Growing a garden became an exercise in faith, patience and ultimately – love. Tending to the little seedlings that slowly grew into large plants filled my heart with hope and optimism for my future. As Will said in his acceptance speech for the Oslo Business for Peace Award: "I've learned that it's not just what you plant, but how you plant it that brings long - term rewards in life, work and the garden."

One afternoon in early August, as I brought in a basket of ripe red tomatoes still warm from the sun, the thought suddenly came to me: gardens grow from grit. All my life experiences had brought me to this point. The good and the bad, the beautiful and the ugly, all played a part in making me who I was. The tough times had strengthened me and prepared me for what lay ahead.

For the first time in years, I allowed myself to just be. In the same way that land is left fallow for a season to prepare it for an amazing harvest the next, I found that by not immediately responding to the world around me and allowing it to dictate my next steps, I allowed my true self to emerge.

I started reading books I had bought years ago and had never opened. I began working out regularly. I began cooking healthy meals with homegrown ingredients. I took my daughter to the playground, reveling in being fully present with her and not glued to a phone screen. My husband and I would sit out on our back deck, drinking endless cups of tea and just enjoying each other's company. I had missed out on all these simple pleasures that now brought so much joy and fullness to my life!

During this time, I also got clear on a key question. What kind of life do I actually want? By this, I don't mean extrinsic material objects like a house, a fancy car, or expensive vacations to far locales. I mean getting clarity on the intrinsic values that, in turn, help shape a life externally. Once I asked myself this question and answered with truth and purpose fueling me, the answer that came was stunning in its simplicity. I wanted to live a life where I used my skills to serve a purpose larger than myself, to earn an income to comfortably support my family, and to have time freedom to do what I wished with my loved ones. That's it. The answer filled me with joy. Now that I was ruthlessly clear on what I stood for, I then proceeded to say "no" to everything that did not support the kind of life I wanted to design. As Joshua Becker says, "The first step in crafting a life you want is to get rid of everything you don't."

Simon Sinek in his seminal book *Start With Why* says that most people don't know why they do what they do. Conversely, people don't buy what you do but why you do what you do. Still with me? What motivated you to do what you have done in your career up to now? Was it the money? Was it the ability to take care of your responsibilities? Whatever it is, it does not have to be at odds with the work you do each day. It is possible (because I am living proof of it!) to align your purpose with your passion and live it every single day.

While I was still unclear about what I would do next, three non-negotiables rose to the surface for what I was no longer willing to do. In this next grand chapter of my life, my work would have to:

1. Be squarely in my zone of genius.

Each of us have what I call "super powers". These are strengths and skills that are uniquely ours. When we utilize these super powers, we are in a state of "flow". Work feels effortless. For so many years, I was only allowed to take certain parts of myself to work. I had to leave other parts at home – those parts that did not fit whatever organizational culture I was in. When we operate from a self that is less than whole, the results we get are inevitably less than whole. Slowly dissociating from our truth and purpose, we become shadows. The end-result? A life that is hollow on the inside.

2. Support the kind of lifestyle I wanted.

We have one daughter and I wanted to be able to spend time with her, to travel when I wanted to, to take off on an impromptu picnic on a Tuesday morning if that's what I wanted! When our internal purpose aligns with the external world that we have created for ourselves, we bring a joy to our work every day that is like nothing else! Interestingly, as I have now discovered, that joy then spreads and permeates to every other part of our lives as well!

3. Entail working with people I liked, trusted, and respected.

While this sounds like a no-brainer, think of all the people we have to work with because our jobs require it. Imagine how much time we spend at work each day. We spend more time with work colleagues than we do with our own family. How often have you returned home from work angry and frustrated with your colleagues or boss and felt that energy taint everything you then did with your family? So doesn't it make sense that we work with people we like, trust, and respect?

What You Seek Is Seeking You

As I got clear on my why and what, the "how" started to appear and my path magically unfolded before me. Then, during that deeply introspective journey somewhere, I discovered the world of franchises. I found that there exists a way to create a life of profit, purpose, and passion.

As a franchise coach, I own my own business. This work is my calling. I wake up every morning excited and grateful for another day to provide value to others and do work I love! I utilize my strengths and gifts every day in the service of my clients. My work has allowed me to create the lifestyle I want. I set my hours and work around family responsibilities and obligations. As long as I have my laptop and my phone, I can work from anywhere in the world – and I have! I only work with people that I want to work with. Before I take someone on as a client, I have them go through a rigorous vetting process to see if we are a fit to work together. If you remember, these were the three non-negotiables that I had set for myself. It was only by being brutally honest with myself that I was able to create the life that I now live.

I don't just help my clients find their "perfect fit" franchise; I help them move from career burnout to career love! I have worked with countless clients, who just like me, were seeking something for which they did not have a name. They were hungering for more purpose, more security, more time, more joy, more *life*.

While every client who comes to me asks, "Can you help me find the franchise that is right for me?" they are actually seeking something even more intrinsic than that. Every client is searching for a way to create a career that they love. This, in turn, helps them create a life that they love.

- Are there moments in your life when you feel unfulfilled?
- Do you feel as though you are caught in a life that no longer fits who you are?
- Do you look at where you are and wonder how you got there?
- Every time you feel this discomfort, do you quickly shove it aside?

If you have answered yes to all these questions, know that you are not alone. I know these feelings all too well myself. Every one of my clients lived with these feelings for a long time until they decided to do something about it.

When do you stop living the status quo to courageously answer the call to do something else?

If you are still reading, then I know that this yearning is in you! If you picked up this book, it is because it called to you. As your franchise coach, I understand your pain because I lived that way too. I now live a life that I designed with intention, filled with the joy of serving others by using my strengths.

Mary Oliver asks in one of her famous poems, "Tell me, what is it you plan to do with your one wild and precious life?" If you have asked yourself this question time and again and feel that your time has passed, then you are wrong. No matter how many years you have spent in the corporate world or how much time you have spent doing something to keep others happy at the expense of your own joy, this moment is the beginning of your new life.

As your franchise coach, I will be beside you as you cross the abyss – the place where you know in your heart that one door has closed and another is yet to open.

Shall we explore what is on the other side?

3

The Six-Step Process for Finding the Franchise That Is Right for You

*"**Metanoia** (n.) the journey of changing one's mind, heart, self, or way of life; spiritual conversion."*

If you are still reading, that tells me that you are seriously looking for a franchise – not just any old franchise, but the one that is right for *you*!

There are currently more than 3,200 franchises in over one hundred categories! From food to retail, education to fitness, beauty to home services, the choices are as diverse as they are overwhelming. With so many options to choose from, how do you find your perfect fit – the one franchise business that fits who you are - your skills and personality, and where you want to go - your goals and desires?

Finding your perfect fit franchise is a process – and you have to understand and follow each step in order to have a successful outcome. Outlined below are the six steps of the proven process I have used with hundreds of clients to help them find the franchise that is right for them. In this chapter, I will outline each step. In subsequent chapters, I will go through each step in detail so you understand the purpose of each step, the work you should be doing, and optimal outcomes.

Each step builds on the one that comes before it, so they should be done in order.

Step 1: Conduct Your Personal Franchise Analysis

Know thyself. These words from the ancient Greek are as relevant today as they were centuries ago when they were uttered by the Oracle of Delphi. Before you can know what business is the right one for you, you must be clear about who you are and what you are.

As a professional in the workplace, when was the last time you took an honest inventory of who you are? As you begin the process of searching for a franchise that is right for you, you will begin by doing a Personal Franchise Analysis.

To begin your Personal Franchise Analysis, start by asking yourself these questions below. Write out the answers that come to your mind. Be as detailed as you want.

- What are your skills and strengths?
- What are those things that put a sparkle in your eye?

- What comes naturally to you?
- What are your weaknesses and blind spots?
- What feels like pulling teeth?
- What are those things that you drag your feet on, that you would happily pay someone else to do for you?

Your answers will paint a picture of all the skills you do (and don't) bring to the table. Different franchises require different strengths, and you need to understand how your strengths (skill sets) align with a specific franchise model.

If you become a franchisee in a franchise system that requires skills that are weaknesses for you, how likely are you to be a successful business owner? Let's say that you became the owner of a franchise that required you, the business owner, to make ten cold calls each day to generate business. You happen to be someone who has never cold-called and is deathly afraid of calling up total strangers. How do you think you will do on your cold calls every day? How successfully will you grow your business using cold-calling as the primary tactic to generate clients? Over the long term, is this a business that you will enjoy growing? In such a scenario, every day becomes a slog. You feel depleted as though you are pushing a large boulder up a hill.

If instead you are a franchisee in a business that requires the skills that are in your zone of genius, you become unstoppable! Every day is another day to get closer to your goals while enjoying the process of getting there! This is where you want to be!

If you are working with a great franchise coach, she will guide you through this critical first step. Don't underestimate the importance of this step. It may seem trivial, but I assure you that it is not.

Step 2: Build Your Franchise Business Model

Your business model is a detailed picture of your perfect fit franchise. It includes all the details of a business that are important to you. Your franchise coach will build your business model in consultation with you.

There are more than 3,200 franchises in the United States alone and they are all very different. Some are home-based while others are brick-and-mortar businesses. Some require hands-on management, while others semi-absentee ownership. Some need only a handful of employees while others can only grow with a large team. There are some franchises that are open every day, 365 days a year while others are only open during regular business hours. These details make up the business models of different franchises.

Using the personal assessment from Step 1 and your business model built by your franchise coach, you can start to narrow down options and see which types of franchises might be a fit and which types to cross off your list. Your business model will include the details that you want and need to be successful. Once you and your coach have built your business model, it should closely approximate the business models of the franchises that are selected for you.

Step 3: Begin Due Diligence with Franchises

Armed with the results of your Personal Franchise Analysis and your Franchise Business Model, you are now ready to begin the process referred to in the franchise industry as "due diligence."

In this step, your franchise coach introduces you to a handful of franchises that she has selected based on your personal analysis and your business model. These franchises may be a fit based on your personal, financial and lifestyle goals as you outlined them in Steps 1 and 2.

Once you begin the process of due diligence with franchises, each franchise will review the major components of their business model with you including customer acquisition, lead generation, marketing, business development, technology platforms, operations, human resources, etc.

Each franchise will also share their Franchise Disclosure Document (FDD) with you. This legal document is presented to prospective franchisees and is comprised of twenty-three items or sections. These items contain detailed information about the franchise system, the franchisor's management team, litigation history, earnings claims, and your legal rights and obligations as a franchisee.

Step 4: Continue Due Diligence with Franchisees

At this stage, you are well into due diligence and are learning the different aspects of the franchises that you are investigating. You now have a better understanding of the different business models, their competitive advantages, and value proposition. You have also done an in-depth review of their Franchise Disclosure Document and have gotten your questions answered.

In this step, you enter the "validation" phase of due diligence. Every franchise that you are speaking to will now introduce you to current franchisees in their system.

During validation, you speak with franchisees of the franchise system you are investigating to get a granular feel for what it is really like to run a particular business. You will be able to ask questions and understand what daily life at a company is really like. No one understands the day-to-day challenges and opportunities of running that particular business better than the franchisees. Speaking to franchisees will be the most invaluable part of your research in helping you determine whether a franchise is the right one for you or not.

Step 5: Fund Your Franchise

As part of building your business model, your franchise coach will review your financials and your desired investment range for the business. As soon as you begin investigating franchise options, your franchise coach will concurrently introduce you to a franchise funding partner to begin the process of figuring out how to fund your franchise once you have found it. There are numerous options, some that may be suitable for you and others that may not, based on an analysis of your specific financial situation.

There are a number of funding options used to start a franchise including SBA loans, 401(k) rollovers, unsecured lines of credit, term loans, and others. Working with a funding professional, you will be able to make the best decision on how to fund your franchise in a way that makes most sense for you.

Step 6: Closeout Due Diligence – Attend Discovery Day & Make a Decision

As you get to the end of the validation phase with franchisees, the franchise will extend a formal invitation to you to meet with them at a Discovery Day. This marks the end of your due diligence.

Discovery Days are regularly held at a franchise's corporate headquarters. These are opportunities for a company to interview the potential candidate (you) and determine if there is a good fit. This is also an opportunity for you to learn more about the company and the team – your extended work family for years to come. You will meet the CEO of the brand who, in many instances, may also be the founder. In speaking with them, you will be able to ask questions to get a better understanding of the "soul" of the business and why they started the company. You will also meet the rest of the executive and operational teams. These are the people who will work closely with you on any issues you have, helping to troubleshoot and course correct as you begin and grow your business.

After attending a Discovery Day, if you like the franchise and they like you, the franchise will formally invite you to become a part of their franchisee family. They will present you with the Franchise Agreement, which is the legal binding contract that lays out the responsibilities of each party: the franchisor - the franchise company, and you - the franchisee.

If you have done your research diligently to understand the business and its potential, you will be in a position to make a decision. Either you will be ready to move forward into ownership, or you will know why you did not. The decision to move forward must sit comfortably on an emotional, business, and financial level. With the help of your franchise coach and your own hard work, you have now found your perfect fit franchise!

If after attending Discovery Day you still don't feel that this is the right business for you, thank the franchise for their time and close out the process. At this point, you have gotten an incredible education in what you don't want. Armed with this valuable information, your franchise coach will present other franchise options that are a better fit with you and your goals. Remember, the search for the perfect fit franchise is more an art than a science. It is an iterative process that gets continuously refined as you move forward.

Before you sign on the dotted lines, your franchise coach will advise you to get the franchise agreement reviewed by a franchise attorney. While this is your personal choice, I would absolutely urge you to engage the services of an attorney who will review your agreement. Before you enter into an agreement with your franchise, you want to be aware of your roles, responsibilities, and obligations as a franchisee. After all, you are entering into a ten-year agreement (in most cases) with a company; don't you want to know what you are signing up for?

Dare to Live the Life You've Always Wanted!

So, what are you thinking? Do the six steps feel over-whelming? Are you having second thoughts about whether you can successfully navigate the search process? Feeling some anxiety is normal and is what makes you human! There should also be a sense of excitement alongside the uncertainty of embarking on a process that you have never before undertaken – excitement for starting a journey into entrepreneurship, at an attempt to write your own future!

I have seen far too many would-be entrepreneurs who never go on to realize their dreams because of fear. The fear of failure, of losing money, of being successful and how that would change their lives…

The franchise search process that I have outlined in this book and that I have led hundreds of clients through is set up for you to succeed. If you do the due diligence to understand the industry and the business and get clear about your role and responsibility as a franchisee, chances are that you *won't* fail. You increase your chances of success because a franchise is a business model that requires you to follow their proven playbook. If you work with a franchise coach who is an industry expert, you will significantly reduce your search time and increase your probability of finding the franchise that is right for you.

Remember what awaits on the other side of your fear: a life you love, work you enjoy, wealth generation, and the freedom to spend time with the ones who matter most to you.

Be brave with your life! If you have been feeling dissatisfied with your career for years and have wondered if there was something better out there – then explore franchise ownership as a career option. You will be so glad that you did!

Step 1 – Conduct Your Personal Franchise Analysis

"The unexamined life is not worth living."
– Socrates

If you are like most of my clients, you think that your search process will begin with you immediately looking at various franchise businesses. While you will eventually do this, it is not the place where you will begin. Think of your search process as moving from the inner (introspective) to the outer (outward-looking) world. Your inner world, in this case, represents your thoughts and motivations, your goals and desires, for why you want to buy a franchise. The first step in the process begins with getting a better understanding of you and your motivations, your strengths and weaknesses, your likes and dislikes. These, in turn, will inform the kinds of franchises (the outer world) that will be best for you in order to achieve your goals.

Make sense? Your search moves from inner to outer.

As you begin this search process for the franchise that is right for you, Step 1 begins by getting a deeper understanding of *you* and your motivations, your inner world that dictates your decisions and actions.

Here are the seven key questions to begin to ask yourself.

1. If you've been an employee throughout your entire career, why are you considering buying a franchise now?

In our society today, shows like *Shark Tank* and *The Profit* make entrepreneurship seem sexy and glamorous. It is often highlighted in movies as the option of choice to make a lot of money. You are the boss and make all the rules, all the while jet-setting around the world on vacations. As a serial entrepreneur, I am here to tell you that while those things can be part and parcel of owning your own business, the reality is a little different. It's not all glam all the time!

Starting a business is no small feat. It will require everything you have and then some! The first six to twelve months of starting a business are the most critical. You will have to put in long hours, learn new skills, overcome your fears. You will need to get really good at managing your time and energy. You will doubt yourself and have to discipline yourself to press forward in spite of it. As prepared as you think you are, you will experience unexpected challenges that you could never have prepared for. Entrepreneurship is hard, hard work.

Being a franchisee is one of the hardest things you will ever do. It will also, however, be one of the most personally and professionally satisfying things you will ever do.

Before All Else, Know Thyself

After spending a lifetime in the telecommunications industry, James was laid off by his employer. He was fifty-two years old, had done well financially, and was jarred by the shock of a lay-off. He felt betrayed. All those years of loyalty to his employer seemed to mean nothing in the end. It shook his self-confidence. It made him question himself, and that made him angrier. As he embarked on a job search, he experienced firsthand that ageism in the corporate world was well and alive. Few companies wanted to pay him the salary he had commanded in his previous position but were eager to get his expertise at a steep discount. After long conversations with his wife, they decided that the corporate world was no longer the answer for them. Franchise ownership was the option that would allow them to create the kind of lifestyle they wanted coupled with the security of never having to be laid off ever again.

James began working with me, and I started him off by getting him clear on why he wanted to start a business of his own. Of course, he needed to make money. Everyone does. In my work with clients, however, I have found that for most individuals it is never just about making money. There is always something else, something more that drives their desire to become an entrepreneur.

I wanted to discover the driving force behind James's desire to become a franchisee. As we peeled back the layers of the onion, I discovered in James someone with an impressive skillset acquired over the years. I also discovered a deep streak of servant leadership. James and his wife were active members of their church. He wanted to be able to run and grow a business that was financially lucrative while providing a service of value to the community. His top two internal motivating factors, as I discovered, were financial security and service to others.

James eventually went on to become a successful franchisee with one of the leading senior care brands in the country. His skillset coupled with his desire to provide a service of value made this particular franchise the winning choice for him. Once he found his perfect fit franchise, he was prepared to get the business off the ground and ready to do what needed to be done to be successful.

 Franchise Pro Tip: Being clear-headed about who you are and why you are embarking on this path makes the eventual journey easier to navigate. When your personal reasons for starting a business are crystal clear and you are focused, your search for your perfect fit franchise becomes that much easier.

2. Why do I want to start a franchise?

Every client who has ever worked with me says that they want to buy a franchise to increase their income. They view the business as a vehicle for wealth generation. Seems logical! Why else would anyone start a business?

Having said that, there are also additional reasons why so many corporate executives look at franchise ownership as a career alternative to the corporate world. While these reasons may not be so readily apparent, they may be equally as important as income generation, if not more.

Let me tell you the story of Denise to illustrate what I mean.

Get Clear on Your "Why"

For over thirty years, Denise had run a very successful management consulting firm in her hometown of Milan, Italy. A year before she attended my workshop where we met, a family emergency had forced her to close her business and move to the U.S. to support her daughter in raising her two young children.

When she began working with me, she explained that she was looking for a business that would provide her with two specific things. First, she had worked her entire adult life and had derived great professional satisfaction from her career. At heart, she knew that she would never retire. After the sudden move to the U.S., however, she felt that she had become a full-time granny and nanny. While she loved the time with her grandchildren, she felt the familiar hunger for something professional. At the same time that she wanted to start another business in the U.S., she needed flexibility to provide childcare during the early afternoon hours while her daughter was still at work.

Using these two very clear needs as guideposts, Denise went on to investigate several franchise businesses. She eventually chose a children's tutoring franchise. It was a perfect fit with what she was looking for: a business model that offered the business owner flexibility in their schedule while providing the professional work that Denise was looking for.

 Franchise Pro Tip: Starting a business is hard work, so understand why you want to start a franchise.

Is it the income potential that is attractive to you? Has your current salary hit a ceiling and you see no room for growth? For most clients, the income potential of a franchise is one of the most compelling reasons for entrepreneurship. When you start your own business, your financial upside is only limited by the time and effort you put into it.

Many clients come to me looking for a business that will provide them with greater work-life balance. They have spent decades in careers that gave them no time with their families, and they are ready to live a more meaningful and personally satisfying life.

Others still are looking for lifestyle flexibility – a career that allows them to work on their schedules and take time off when they want to. If you have young children or older parents that you are responsible for, owning your own business may give you the work-life balance that you have been searching for. This kind of flexibility is almost impossible to achieve when holding down a job as an employee.

Whatever your "why", get clear on it so that you are one step closer to the franchise that will be right for you!

Here are the top ten reasons my clients chose to start a franchise:

- Create greater wealth
- Take control of their destiny
- Build an asset over time that can be sold for a profit
- Be their own boss
- Make a difference in the lives of others
- Build, mentor, and lead a team
- Create a life of purpose
- Create a family business
- Receive a better return on investment (ROI) on capital (as compared to the stock market)
- Create a legacy that lives on after they are gone

Whatever your reasons are for investigating franchises, becoming clear about them will help you to pinpoint and home in on those franchises whose models allow you to create the life and lifestyle you want. Remember, this is your business. It must fit your life. Not the other way around!

3. Do I understand what it means to be a business owner?

A franchise is often referred to as a "business in a box." It offers a proven business model and a playbook for franchisees to follow. A franchise, through its systems, also provides its franchisees with a quicker start-up. Working with an established franchise and a network of franchisees ensures that you are in business "for" yourself but never in business "by" yourself. Despite all these advantages, a franchisee still has to do the work. They will have to understand the playbook and implement it in order to grow the business. They will have to learn the systems of the franchisor. They must do local marketing to create awareness and business development to acquire clients. There is much work to be done. A franchise is an excellent option for many, but it is not a magic wand. Becoming a franchisee does not automatically guarantee success.

The question to ask yourself is: am I willing to do the hard work needed to get my business off the ground and grow it?

As Lori Greiner of *Shark Tank* says, "Entrepreneurs are willing to work eighty hours a week to avoid working forty hours a week." Is this you? Will you do what it takes to take care of your baby, A.K.A. your business? Because if you don't, it will fail.

From Employee to Entrepreneur

Originally from Argentina, Nate moved to the United States as a teenager. Over two decades, he built a successful career in the automotive industry, growing and honing his skill set. When he came to me, he was standing at a crossroads, looking for an opportunity that would allow him to use his business talents and prior success to create wealth and security for himself and his family.

Nate was very clear-headed. He understood that the move from employee to entrepreneur would take everything he had. He was focused and determined. He went through the search process with intention.

When the time came, he decided to move forward with a residential cleaning franchise. He felt the brand's support system was exactly what he needed as a first-time entrepreneur. During his due diligence, he had focused on understanding the kind and level of support he would receive from them. Being a business owner for the first time, he wanted to ensure his probability of success would be as high as possible.

Once he formally became a franchisee, he moved aggressively to secure a location for his office, hired employees, and went through all the different aspects of start-up to get set up for success. Despite numerous unforeseen obstacles along the way, Nate continued to keep his "eyes on the prize". In an industry known for poor customer service, he has built a business that has established its reputation in the local community for going above and beyond and exceeding client expectations. This is the direct result of his dogged determination to succeed at being an entrepreneur.

 Franchise Pro Tip: Ultimately, entrepreneurship is an act of self-determination. Every single client of mine who went on to start a franchise felt they had the drive in them to do everything they needed to succeed in their business. When considering going from an employee to an entrepreneur, you must thoroughly do the due diligence on the business and its model. Once you have done so and determined that the business is indeed the right one for you, you must have a certain level of self-confidence in your own capabilities that you will succeed no matter what.

4. Am I willing to follow the franchisor's playbook?

One major reason that franchisees fail in their business is their inability or unwillingness to follow their franchisor's system. As a franchisee, you have paid the franchise to be a part of their system. These are systems that are proven and time-tested. If you won't use their Standard Operating Protocols (SOPs), then why are you paying for it?

From time to time, I will have some workshop attendees say to me that they no longer want a boss, even if that boss is a playbook that has to be followed. My response to them is simple: a franchise is not the right option for you!

The Quickest Way to Fail in a Franchise is to Ignore Their System

When I first met Jason, I was impressed by his quiet determination and focus. He was a young man of twenty-two and had lived a hard life. Shaped by a turbulent childhood, he felt that the only way to succeed and provide for his family was through a business of his own. Over the course of a couple of months, I worked with Jason to investigate different brands and help him find the right franchise. Jason ended up becoming one of the youngest franchisees ever of a very well-known home remodeling company.

This particular franchise is known in the industry for its best-in-class franchisee training and robust systems. I was confident that Jason was going to blow everyone out of the water and become a top performing franchisee in a couple of years. Barely two years into it, however, he parted ways with the company. After being with the franchise for less than six months, he started butting heads with management and questioning their pricing structures, among other things. As a result of his unwillingness to follow the playbook, his business never really took off. He struggled until finally he made the decision to part ways with the franchise.

 Franchise Pro Tip: If you are unwilling to follow your franchisor's playbook, you will not be successful.

Before you make the decision to buy a franchise, ask yourself these two hard questions. As you answer, make sure you are being honest with yourself.

1. Are you okay with following directions in order to be successful?

A franchise is a proven business. It is proven because there are franchisees around the country (if it is a domestic brand) or around the world (if is a global brand) who have become successful by following the brand's systems. As part of your due diligence, you will be speaking with numerous franchisees. During this phase of your search, try to get an understanding of how closely they are expected to follow the franchise's playbook. Do they have some leeway in how they operate their business or not? Remember, if you become a franchisee with this brand, you will be expected to follow the same playbook.

You are going to be paying royalties to the franchise over the life of your contract with them. This is in exchange for their system and their ongoing support. If you are not going to use their system, you are better off starting a business from scratch.

2. Do you need to be the one in charge all the time?

A franchise will give you more independence and freedom than a job ever will. Having said that, you will still have to follow your franchise's directions and guidance to be successful. If this chafes at you and you don't want another boss even if it is in the guise of a playbook, then a franchise is probably not the best option for you.

5. Do I have what it takes to be successful?

As you progress through the search process, there is a specific step called "validation." During validation, you speak to franchisees of the businesses that your franchise coach has picked out for you. In speaking with them, you should try to get an understanding of not just how they did what they did but *who* they are as business owners.

Are all the franchisees outgoing and gregarious? Do they enjoy meeting new people? Are they all doing a lot of networking to grow their business? If all the owners in a brand that you speak to have this personality trait and you don't, this business may not be the right fit for you.

Success Looks Different for Different People

Susan had just started validation with franchisees. Among the franchises that I had given her, one was a home services franchise. In her conversations with franchisees, she realized that the background and personality of a vast majority of franchisees were like hers.

Many were vets. They understood what it meant to follow a system, execute for results, and lead a team. They were sociable people who liked networking. They were service-oriented leaders. Providing a service of value to their community ranked high in their professional goals. As she dug deeper, it became clear to her that this was indeed her tribe. Because there were so many similarities between her and the franchisees that she spoke to, she felt that her probability of success in this business would be high.

Susan went on to become a franchisee with this business, one of the most reputable and well-known home services franchise in the industry. She could see her own success in the franchisees that she validated with and felt confident that this was her perfect fit franchise.

 Franchise Pro Tip: As you ask yourself whether you have what it takes to be a successful franchisee, start to make a list of what you believe are your strengths and talents.

- What are those things that you are known for by your colleagues?

- What is a task that your boss always comes to you for because no one else does it as well as you do?
- Have you led a large team of people to accomplish big projects for your company?
- Do you understand operations like the back of your hand?
- Are you a whiz at marketing?
- Do you consistently hit the sales target for your team?
- Are you successful at closing sales with clients?
- Are you skilled at handling customer complaints and converting disgruntled clients into returning clients?

Whatever your "superpowers" are, this is the time to make a list of them. This list will become handy as you begin to look at various franchises and understand what skills they require of their franchisees. Remember that your superpowers will bring you success in your chosen franchise. Your list of superpowers will also be incorporated into the business model that your franchise coach prepares for you.

6. Do I have the financial resources needed?

Buying a franchise is both an emotional decision as well as a financial one. Before you begin, do an inventory of your financials. This, too, is part of the initial assessment that your franchise coach will help you with.

Make a list of all your assets and your liabilities.

Your assets can include:

- Cash (checking and savings)

- Stocks, bonds, CDs
- Home market value
- Retirement accounts – 401(k), IRA
- Automobiles
- Personal property
- Any money due to you
- Pension
- Any other assets

Your liabilities can include:
- Credit card debt
- Auto debt
- Mortgage outstanding
- Line of credit
- Accounts payable
- Any other debts

The first twelve months of the business are the most important in determining its long-term success and viability. Many new businesses go under because they do not have the additional resources needed for an unexpected situation. Understanding how much in assets you have before you start will give you peace of mind. You should also think through and ask yourself if you have access to extra resources should you need them. If you do not have them, do you have family or friends who will be willing to help you out? What other options may be available?

During your validation calls with successful franchisees, you will begin to get a very good understanding of how much money you will need to cover your living expenses before your business becomes profitable. It is essential for you to have a cash cushion for emergencies. One strategy that many of my married clients use is to decide to have one spouse be responsible for running the franchise full-time while the other spouse remains in their full-time job. The job continues to bring in a monthly income which serves as the cash cushion until the business becomes profitable. Once the business becomes profitable, the spouse may choose to leave their job to pitch into the business and grow it at an even faster pace.

During your search process, you will also be given the Franchise Disclosure Document (FDD) by each franchise that you investigate. The FDD is a legal document that every franchise has to file with the Federal Trade Commission to remain in good standing. This document, typically several hundred pages long will, among other things, give you an idea of the start-up costs associated with a particular business. This will give you a good handle on how much money you need to invest to get going and how much to keep on hand for emergencies, should they arise.

Risk is the Down Payment on Success

Colin and Tammy are a successful professional couple. Colin was the Vice President of Business Development for his company. Tammy was the Vice President of Finance for her organization. When they came to me, they were both working in their full-time positions. While they were about ten years away from retirement, they wanted to find a franchise that they could start immediately to begin building a stream of income for their golden years.

After looking at several brands, they decided to move forward with a business that provided indoor and outdoor signage for companies. They made the decision that Colin would leave his job to work in the business full-time. Tammy would remain in her job until the business stabilized and started bringing in an income. With this game plan, they felt they would be able to ride the risk better by having one person bring in a stable income until their business became profitable.

 Franchise Pro Tip: If you are married or have a partner, discuss how each person will be involved in the business. Will you take an active role in starting and growing the business? If both of you are currently employed, do you both leave your jobs? Or does just one of you?

If the franchise you have chosen requires the franchisee to be an "owner operator", one of you will have to take on the role to run the business full-time. If, however, the franchise can be run "semi-absentee", then you have the flexibility of continuing in your current job while starting the business. For semi-absentee businesses, you also have the flexibility of hiring a manager to take on your role.

Being clear about the roles you will each take on once you have found the business will make the first twelve months that much easier to navigate and increase your probability of success.

Many franchisees have failed in their business not because of a lack of trying or because the franchise was not a robust model but because they did not have the extra cash to cover expenses when the need arose.

There are franchises available at every investment level. Your franchise coach will help in identifying those businesses whose investment levels do not over-leverage you. You should ideally get into a franchise that you can comfortably afford.

You Don't Need to Spend a Million Bucks to Make a Million Bucks!

When I met David at my franchise workshop, he was working as a security officer at a federal prison facility. As a teenager, he had come to the United States as an immigrant from Latin America. He joined the military and began his career in service. He worked his way up the ranks and was able to provide a comfortable life for his wife and two young children.

After leaving the military, he began a civilian job as a prison security officer. As he described it, the work was dangerous. The inmates were frequently violent. There was one particular incident in which an inmate who had stolen a hypodermic needle attacked David with it when he tried to tackle him. He was shaken. There were better ways to make a living, and he began his search for a business of his own.

When he started working with me, he was very eager to find the right business but felt that he did not have the requisite financials. Like many others, he came to me with the mistaken assumption that you have to spend a lot of money buying a franchise to be able to get a commensurate return from it. In actuality, the cost of a business has very little to do with how much you can make from it. There is no direct correlation between the cost of a franchise and its return.

As with many other clients, he was interested in exploring food franchises that typically cost several hundred thousand dollars to start. His financials, however, did not support the investment level for a restaurant. As I worked with him to clarify his goals, David realized that it was possible for him to make the kind of income he was looking for without spending an arm and a leg. Given his skill sets, I introduced him to several home service brands. During his due diligence process reviewing the FDD and speaking to franchisees, he was astonished to learn how successful franchisees of a particular brand had been and how much money they had invested to get started. The decision was simple. He had found his franchise. As he said to me, "It doesn't cost a million bucks to make a million bucks!" David is now a happy franchisee providing his clients with a service that protects homes and neighborhoods – chimney sweeping.

 Franchise Pro Tip. Once your franchise coach has helped you analyze your financials, schedule a conversation with a franchise funding organization to better understand how much you can comfortably afford. The last thing you want to do is to start a new business and be distracted from growing it because you are worried about the large debt load you have to service each month.

Remember, it does not take a million bucks to make a million bucks! There are franchises available in every investment range. This is the beauty of the franchise industry!

7. Is my family going to be supportive?

Starting a business is a hard thing to do.

Starting a business without the support of your loved ones is almost impossible to do.

Starting a business will require dedicated time and focused energy. Your family must understand and accept the demands that a business will create on you. Involve them from the start and get their buy-in. This may be one of the most important things you do before you begin your search. Once you have started the search, keep them updated on your progress and key aspects of the businesses that you are learning about. As you involve them in every step, they will feel more vested in you and the business and its eventual success.

I cannot underscore the importance of ensuring your spouse or family is on board with you before starting a franchise.

Let me share Paul's story to reiterate the importance of this.

You Cannot Go It Alone

Paul attended a franchise workshop that I was leading for corporate executives who had been laid off from their jobs. As a C-suite executive, he had enjoyed a very successful career in the U.S. and Europe working for large reputable organizations. He was very adept at managing global teams and leading complex projects to their successful conclusion.

When he began working with me, I asked him as I typically do every person who wants to work with me, if his spouse was on board with his desires to be a franchise owner. He explained that she was not. She did not understand businesses or how they worked and felt that they were too risky. She wanted him to find another corporate job. As he talked about her, I immediately knew this was a red flag. I shared with him why I did not think it was a good idea to begin unless she was also willing to get on at least one call with me. He assured me that this would not be necessary and that she would "eventually come around."

As Paul progressed with his due diligence, he shared the different questions that his wife had on the businesses that I had given him. She was clearly worried that he was making the wrong decision by even investigating them. Two months into his due diligence process, just as I had predicted, he told me that he would not be moving forward. He had a long talk with his wife. In order to preserve the peace in his marriage, he had decided that a job would better serve the needs of their family.

Several months later, Paul returned to the corporate world.

 Franchise Pro Tip. Get your cheerleader, be they spouse or significant other, on board *before* you decide to begin your franchise search. Trust me, you will avoid a lot of heartache and misunderstanding with your loved ones if you do so.

In many instances, I have had clients whose spouses had no interest in being involved in a business. However, as the client progressed through the search and updated them on what they were learning and which business they were starting to lean into, their spouses not only became more involved but eventually ended up working alongside them in the business in significant ways.

Am I Ready to Start Investigating Franchises That Are Right for Me?

Try to answer these questions in as much detail as you can. Every client I have ever worked with were like onions! As I took them through the search process, I peeled off layer after layer to get to the heart of the business they were looking for. Do the same with yourself now.

Clarify why you are undertaking the franchise search process now. Take some time to go over each question and answer honestly. This exercise, done at the start, will help you avoid costly mistakes down the road. Working with a reputable franchise coach, who serves as your guide and sounding board, will also help you ask the right questions.

Are you still with me? Fantastic!

In the next chapter, we will go over the franchise business model – what it is, the three key components, and why this tool is the critical blueprint for your franchise search. The more accurate your business model is, the greater the likelihood that your franchise coach will be able to introduce you to franchises that are a fit with what you are looking for.

5

Step 2 – Create Your Franchise Business Model

"Luck is not a business model."
– Anthony Bourdain

"Will I be successful in a franchise business?"

If you have never owned a business before, then this question looms large in your mind. While there are many factors that will ultimately determine your success or failure in a franchise, I have found through my work with clients that there is one key component that, if absent, can dramatically skyrocket your probability of failure. I call this the fit. Fit – it is a tiny word with huge implications for your success or failure as a business owner.

Whatever the business is, it must be one that fits you. What do I mean by this?

The franchise you choose must be a business that builds on your strengths and your skills. Every franchise system has franchisees who are top performers and others who are not doing very well. The system the franchise provides to all of its franchisees is the same. The difference, of course, is the franchisee. Each franchisee has unique skills and strengths, weaknesses and blind spots. They come in with varying backgrounds – some spent their entire careers in the corporate world while others were serial entrepreneurs. They are diverse in their age, race, and gender.

Take this simple example as an illustration of how critical "fit" becomes in your eventual success. Take, as an example, a franchise that requires the franchisee to be adept at networking and public speaking as a way to generate new clients. If the franchisee is shy by nature, is afraid of public speaking and does not enjoy meeting complete strangers, how successful do you think they will be at this business? The answer is: probably not very successful.

As you evaluate franchises that your franchise coach gave you based on your fit, continue asking yourself one question: will I be successful as a franchisee in this business given who I know myself to be? Just because your brother's best friend's niece is successful at a particular franchise does not mean that you will be. The opposite is equally as true.

Have you heard the saying "if you don't know where you are going, you will never get there?"

Step 2 of the search process involves the creation of a detailed picture of a franchise business that meets *your* personal, professional, lifestyle, and financial goals. In order for you to find the franchise that is right for you, you first have to get clear on the details of what you are looking for.

I call this detailed picture: the franchise business model. Your franchise business model is the blueprint of your franchise search. This detailed roadmap, created with the help of your franchise coach, will lay out all the different characteristics that you want your perfect fit franchise to have.

There are three key components to your franchise business model:

1. Your Franchise Superpowers
2. Your Franchise Goals
3. Your Franchise Preferences

Your Franchise Superpowers

In Chapter 4, you asked yourself if you had what it took to be successful as a franchisee.

What superpowers did you make in that list? Are you a marketing maven? Do you handle customer issues like no one else? Are you a ninja when it comes to your attention to details? Are you constantly admired for your project management skills? Are you skilled at building and nurturing relationships? Are you an authentic and effective networker?

Pull that list out now. In your franchise business model, you will start to align your skills and strengths with specific businesses that require those skills.

Your Franchise Goals

Very simply, your franchise goals represent your "wish list" for your franchise. Your goals are your personal reasons for why you want to go into business for yourself.

Remember the exercise you did in Chapter 4?

What did you list as your key reasons for starting a franchise? Was it financial independence? Was it flexibility to spend more time with your kids? Was it a desire for work that was more personally meaningful to you? Where do you want to be in five, ten, twenty years?

Also think about the types of things that you want to avoid.

Have you always been an "individual contributor" in your job? Do you prefer working by yourself over working with a team? How long do you want your commute to ideally be? Do you want a business that allows you to be outside and does not require hours every day in front of a computer? Do you enjoy managing and leading others? Or do you try to avoid it like the plague?

Whatever your franchise goals are, this is the place to list them. Be clear, be bold, be thoughtful. The more clarity you bring to this exercise, the greater will be your motivation to make this a reality and find your fit!

Your Franchise Preferences

Just as you did with your franchise goals, this is a second list you are going to make. Your franchise preferences are the specific role(s) you want to play in your franchise.

Some questions your franchise coach may ask, in this section, include the following:

- Do you want to be a full-time owner-operator and work in the business every day?
- Or do you want to run it semi-absentee by hiring a manager who manages the day-to-day operations, freeing you up to do something else?
- What industry category do you want to be in – food, automotive, retail, business services, personal services, senior care, children, etc.?
- Do you want to serve customers who are individuals (D2C) or businesses (B2B)?
- What hours and days do you want your business to be open? Do you want banker's hours, nine a.m. to five p.m.? Or do you want to be open 24/7, 365 days of the year to be able to capture any and all opportunities?
- How many and what kind of employees do you want?
- Do you prefer a franchise that provides a service versus one that provides a product?
- Do you want a franchise that is professional (business consulting, financial expense reduction, tutoring, etc.) or one that is in the trades (plumbing, painting, home repair, etc.)?

Your superpowers – skills and interests, strengths and talents – should match up with your franchise preferences.

You will use your franchise model to narrow down your search from thousands of franchise options to a small handful, so be deliberate and spend as much time as you need on this exercise.

Also, remember that your franchise business model is not etched in stone. Should any preferences change, you should ask your franchise coach to update your model. Using your franchise model creates a level playing field that allows you to compare very different franchises to ensure that the one you end up choosing will meet all your goals – personal, professional, lifestyle, and financial.

Take a deep breath! You have just completed the foundational work for your franchise search by building your business model. At this stage, if you are working with a franchise coach, she will start introducing you to franchise brands whose business models most closely match *your* business model.

As Meister Eckhart said, "And suddenly, you know… it's time to start something new and trust the magic of new beginnings."

Are you ready?

Let's begin the journey to find your perfect fit franchise!

6

Step 3 – Begin Due Diligence with Franchises

"If you want to go somewhere, it is best to find someone who has already been there."
– Robert Kiyosaki

Congratulations!

Working with your franchise coach, you have now completed your personalized franchise business model. Are you starting to get some clarity around what sorts of franchises may be a potential fit for you? Conversely, are you also able to picture what businesses may not work for you in helping you attain your goals? Great! This is exactly what your model should be helping you do!

With your franchise business model in hand, you are now ready to start your search process, also known as due diligence. Your franchise coach has hand-picked several franchises for you to investigate because they meet the criteria of what you are looking for. Your coach will personally introduce you to the management team at these franchises. Each franchise will then reach out to you to begin the search process. Keep in mind that every franchise has a very specific and intentional process of discovery.

Best Practices for Due Diligence

As you begin your due diligence to find your franchise, consider incorporating these best practices into your search process to keep it efficient and to ensure that you are on track.

- The due diligence process is intended for *you*. What you put into it in terms of time and effort is what you will get out of it. If you skate on the surface and don't dig deep, you are unlikely to find your perfect fit franchise. If, on the other hand, you lean in and are curious to learn about different business models, you are in for a treat! You will get an education like no other… and, in the process, discover the franchise that is meant for you!

- Come to this process with an open and curious mind. Be open to learning about franchises that you may never have considered on your own. The beauty of working with a franchise coach is that she will introduce you to businesses that you may never have known or heard about! At first blush, you may not feel much excitement about a business and think that this automatically means that it is not the right one for you. Wrong! I ask my clients to very consciously set aside their preconceived notions of what they think is successful and to be very aware of any stereotypes they may hold. Your decision about which franchise is the right one for you should be based on your research, on facts and figures and conversations with franchisees. Only then can you be sure you are making the best decision.

- When you first begin the search, you will likely want to immediately talk about how much money franchisees are making. Most clients do! While that feels logical   after all, you are investigating businesses for their profitability – that is the wrong approach. Why? In addition to the money-making potential of a franchise, you will want to learn its business model. How do you get clients? How do you market? How do you differentiate yourself from the competition? Learning the business first allows you to make a determination of whether this business is in the ballpark of what is right for you. You should also remember that your franchise coach would never recommend a franchise to you that does not hold the income potential that you are looking for. That is a given. So, start the search process, follow the franchisor's lead, and learn their business model first.

- Schedule at least one call every week with each franchise you are investigating. Every call will be structured to go over one key aspect of the franchise's business model. These will include marketing, operations, site selection, the franchise disclosure document (FDD), hiring employees, and much more. By keeping to this schedule, you should be able to go from start to finish within three months. This is a reasonable timeframe in which to find the franchise that is right for you. If, however, you are not diligent about your weekly research schedule with the brands, you will invariably lose momentum.

- Come to each call prepared. For each franchise you are investigating, start making a list of questions you have. You want to be viewed as a serious candidate and not as a "tire kicker" who is wasting their time.

- After having one call with a brand, you may feel like the brand is absolutely not for you. That's great! Because you are not looking at them through rosy-colored glasses, you will be more objective about your research and the questions you ask. I advise my clients to make at least three calls with each brand before they make the decision to drop one.

- Before each call, you will typically receive some homework to do. These can include videos to watch, brochures to read, applications to fill out, etc. Make sure you are getting these done in a timely manner. I have always said that the way you do anything is the way you do everything. Your professionalism and timely responsiveness throughout this process is being watched very closely by the franchise executive you are working with. While they may never directly say anything to you, you can be sure that they are looking out for behaviors and traits that may be potential red flags in a franchisee.

- When you receive the Franchise Disclosure Document from the franchise, make sure you review it from start to end. Typically, FDDs are boring legal documents that are several hundred pages long. Your first instinct may be to skim through quickly. Don't! Later in the chapter, we will go through a more detailed analysis of each section in the FDD. As you read the FDD, prepare a list of any questions or concerns you have. You want to ensure that all your questions are answered.

- If you know that you are going to miss a call for any reason, be sure to reach out to the franchise executive you are working with beforehand to let them know and reschedule the call. Creating a good impression goes a long, long way. The executives you will be speaking to are professionals with busy schedules, and you want to be respectful of their time.

While some of these best practices might seem like no-brainers, you will be amazed at how many otherwise qualified clients drop the ball, convey the wrong impression, and the process ends with the franchise politely closing out the search process with them. These best practices will ensure that you come across to these brands as a serious and well-prepared candidate and that you track with your research in a timely manner.

When my clients begin the due diligence process, there are two key questions they always have.

These are:

1. When I begin speaking to franchises, what questions should I ask?
2. The FDD feels daunting! Is there anything in particular that I should be looking out for?

Over the years, I have put together resource documents for my clients to help them navigate a search process that can seem overwhelming at times. Below are these two key resources for your own search.

Due Diligence Guide: Key Questions to Ask Franchisors

As you begin your conversation with franchises (also known as franchisors), here is a suggested list of key questions to ask them.

1. How much will it cost to purchase the franchise?

While you will get this number from Item 7 of the FDD (estimated initial investment), you still want to ask the franchise this question. Understand what an average amount is, if there will be any variations given the particular part of the country where you will be opening the business. How much of a cash cushion should you have on hand so you don't run out of capital before your business becomes profitable?

2. What is the background of the company and its executive management team?

While this information, including previous litigation, will be listed in Items 1-3 of the FDD, you want to get a sense of who these people are. Do they have industry experience? Are they qualified to run this company? After all, you are paying them to become a part of their system. You want to know if they have the background to grow the business successfully for years to come.

3. How old and established is the franchise?

How long have they been franchising? How many franchised locations/ franchisees do they currently have? How many franchisees have left their system, if any? Why did they leave?

Ask executives about the evolution of the brand. As they grew, how did they improve over the years? How has that translated into the support they provide their franchisees?

If the franchise is fairly new, what are their plans for growth? How will they help their franchisees succeed? Do they have a plan in place?

4. How successful are the franchisees?

Gather information from the franchise executives, the FDD, and interviews you will have with current franchisees in the system. Does the information from all sources match or is there any discrepancy?

5. What type of support do they offer to their franchisees?

When you become a franchisee, how much ongoing support will you get? Are particular executives assigned to your region? What support will you be able to get from the corporate team? Are there opportunities to meet with the other franchisees at yearly conferences? Are there educational opportunities you will receive as a franchisee?

6. What is their system/ playbook like?

Is theirs a system that is easy to understand and follow? You need to determine if this a system you are capable of following. Also, is the system sufficient to help you achieve success? Sometimes, newer franchises may still be working out the kinks.

7. What support do they provide for a new franchisee who is having difficulties?

Is there a support system of some kind? Are you assigned a coach from the corporate office for the first twelve months of the start-up period? Do they pair you up with a seasoned franchisee in the system who acts as your mentor? Good franchisors should have adequate support to help you during the start-up phase when you may hit a few stumbling blocks and try to navigate unforeseen challenges.

8. How competitive is the market?

It might seem like some business sectors are flooded with competitors. You're wondering if it even makes sense to start a business in that sector. Is the field too crowded, or is that a sign of strong, growing demand? Understand what the franchise considers its competition locally and how they plan to help you succeed in your local market.

9. What activities does the owner spend their time on?

Does the owner of a Burger King flip burgers all day? Of course, not! As you learn about franchises, remember to separate the role of the owner (you) from what the business sells. The two may be very different! In your conversations with the franchise executives, you will want to learn what the franchisee will be responsible for. Do those tasks align with your strengths and skills? If not, do you have flexibility to hire someone who does so you can spend time doing those tasks that are in your zone of genius?

To this guide, feel free to add additional questions that are important or specific to you and your local market.

Reviewing the FDD

Franchising is a highly regulated industry, and oversight is maintained by the Federal Trade Commission (FTC). Complex regulations govern the industry and are intended to protect potential franchisees, like you, who are considering buying a franchise.

To ensure that franchises are giving prospective franchisees the proper amount of information needed to make an educated decision, the FTC mandates that the FDD be provided to the prospective franchisee no later than fourteen days before any binding documents are signed. The fourteen-day period begins with the signing of a formal receipt. The receipt does not establish any obligation on your part; it simply acknowledges that you have received the FDD from the franchisor.

Due Diligence Guide: A Primer on the FDD

The FDD contains twenty-three separate sections or "items," as they are commonly referred to as. While reading the FDD may seem onerous to you, it is one of the key aspects of your research. You will get details on various aspects of the franchise that allow you to get a more comprehensive picture of the business. It is almost impossible to find any other industry where you can get this level of detail and information before making an investment. Take advantage of this. Dig deep and round out your understanding of what made a particular franchise the 800-pound gorilla in its category or why another business grew to several hundred locations in just a couple of years!

Here are the twenty-three items or sections of a FDD:

1. The Franchisor and Any Parents, Predecessors, and Affiliates

Item 1 presents a general review of the company, including any predecessors or affiliates, and the opportunity being offered. This section presents an overview of the business.

2. Business Experience

Item 2 presents background information on key officers, directors, employees and any others who hold management responsibility in the franchise.

3. Litigation

Item 3 covers any and all litigation, both current and past, going back ten years.

4. Bankruptcy

Item 4 discloses any bankruptcies, either on the part of the franchisor or its founder.

5. Initial Fees

Item 5 details any and all initial fees you have to pay as you begin the franchise business.

6. Other Fees

Item 6 details the initial fees associated with becoming a franchisee, including the franchise fee itself, royalty, advertising, renewal, transfer fees, multi-unit fees, and necessary supplies/materials.

7. Estimated Initial Investment

Item 7 covers every component of the total initial investment required, combining the initial fees disclosed in Item 5 with estimates of construction/leasehold improvement costs, furniture, fixtures, equipment, signage, computer systems, rent deposits, insurance deposits, professional fees, grand opening expenses, and any other expenses.

This section is meant to give you a solid estimate of the total cost of opening a franchise location. Review this section with existing franchisees (during the validation phase) and the franchisor to determine the most accurate estimate possible for your specific location and situation.

8. Restrictions on Sources of Products and Services

Item 8 discusses supply sources and ongoing operational items. This specific item becomes particularly important if you are in a food-based concept.

9. Franchisee's Obligations

Item 9 discusses your obligations as a franchisee. Make sure you are clear about your expected responsibilities.

10. Financing

Item 10 describes the terms and conditions of any financing arrangements offered by the franchisor.

11. Franchisor's Assistance, Advertising, Computer Systems, and Training

Item 11 details the contractual support that the franchisor is obligated to provide to you, the franchisee. It tells you what you will receive in exchange for the fees you are paying. The section outlines pre-opening assistance as well as ongoing assistance. It also provides extensive detail about the franchisor's training programs and any required franchise systems, such as computer point of sale or advertising programs.

12. Territory

Item 12 provides the description of any protected or exclusive territory.

Most prospective franchisees believe intuitively that the bigger the protected territory, the better for them. To the contrary, the most successful and well-known franchise systems typically offer territories that are either extremely limited or territories that are not protected at all.

13. Trademarks

Item 13 provides information about the franchisor's trademarks, service, and trade names.

14. Patents, Copyrights, and Proprietary Information

Item 14 gives information about how the brand's patents and copyrights can be used by the franchisee.

15. Obligation to Participate in the Actual Operation of the Franchise Business

Item 15 explains exactly what the franchisee's personal obligations are in relation to the operation of the franchise business.

16. Restrictions on What the Franchisee May Sell

Item 16 deals with any restrictions on the goods and services that the franchisee may offer its customers.

17. Renewal, Termination, Transfer, and Dispute Resolution

Item 17 details when and whether your franchise can be renewed or terminated. It also details your rights and restrictions when you have disagreements with your franchisor.

18. Public Figures

If the franchisor uses public figures (celebrities or public persons), Item 18 discloses how much the person is compensated.

19. Financial Performance Representations

Item 19 details the financial performance of the franchisor's units.

This is often the first item prospective franchisees read to determine the answer to the most commonly asked question in franchising: "How much money can I make in this business?"

Item 19, however, will never give you the answer to this question. In fact, the disclaimers of every Item 19 representation make this point abundantly clear. Every franchisee and every location is different. It is impossible to predict in advance what future financial performance results you might achieve.

What Item 19 does provide, however, are clues that you can use to guide your own research in answering the question of how much money you might make. The key with Item 19 is to be very cautious and use the information within the scope of what it is meant to convey. You will then verify this data in your validation calls with existing franchisees.

This is the reason why the validation phase is the most important part of your search process. By using Item 19 information in conjunction with your validation calls with franchisees, you will be able to make the best determination of how profitable this business can be for *you*.

20. Outlets and Franchisee Information

Item 20 provides locations and contact information of existing franchisees. By reviewing the number of units that have transferred ownership or closed, this section will help you in understanding the growth of the franchise system and success rate of franchisees.

21. Financial Statements

Item 21 details the audited financial statements for the past three years.

22. Contracts

Item 22 provides all the agreements that the franchisee will be required to sign.

All contracts you may be required to execute in conjunction with becoming a franchisee, including the actual Franchise Agreement contract and other contracts covering personal guarantees, real estate assignments, advertising, co-op rules and conditions, and territorial development schedules, will all be included in this section.

23. Receipts

Prospective franchisees are required to sign a receipt that they received the FDD.

If you are looking at a FDD for the first time, it is easy to feel overwhelmed. This document is several hundred pages long and filled with numbers and legalese. The good news here is that you are not expected to digest this tome on your own! Because the FDD is such a critical document in explaining key aspects of the franchise opportunity, the franchisor will spend ample time with you to walk you through the core aspects of the document.

I have also found that once the initial overwhelm passes, my clients appreciate the amount of information that is contained in the FDD. By the time you have reviewed the FDD with the franchisor, you will have a very good understanding of what the FDD entails and what you can expect both in terms of the investment, as well as the support, assistance, and training that you will receive from the franchisor.

Engaging a Franchise Attorney

Because of the myriad legal, operational, and financial details contained within the FDD, I always advise my clients to engage the services of a franchise attorney. I work with some of the most reputable franchise lawyers in the country who understand the legal aspects of this industry like few others. I introduce all clients to a lawyer who can guide them through the FDD to understand their roles and responsibilities as a franchisee within a particular franchise system.

Buying into a franchise is a significant investment – financially, of course, and in other ways. Making sure you know what you are getting into, i.e. being clear about what is contained in the FDD, will go a long way towards ensuring your eventual success as a franchisee. Protect your investment by working closely with an attorney before you make the big decision. I have never yet had a client who regretted getting legal counsel before they made the decision to move forward with the franchise of their choice.

Okay! You have covered a lot of ground in this chapter. You are well into your due diligence process to find the franchise that is a fit with you and your goals.

In the following chapter, we will go over the next step in the due diligence process: validation with franchisees of the brands you are investigating. This is the heart of your search process.

Step 4 – Continue Due Diligence with Franchisees

*"Everyone you will ever meet
knows something that you don't."*
– Bill Nye

In Chapter 6, we went through a detailed overview of the initial steps of your due diligence or search process. First, your franchise coach, upon completing your franchise business model, matched you with a handful of franchises that have the greatest probability of meeting your goals. Second, she introduced you to the executives at each brand to begin your discovery. These franchise executives worked one-on-one with you to guide you through your search with their brand. Third, you began scheduling calls and webinars with each franchise, learning about particular aspects of their business model, including a detailed review of the Franchise Disclosure Document.

You are now ready to begin the next step of the process called "validation." This is possibly the most important part of your search process. Why? These franchisees were in your shoes, went through the same process as you are going through right now, and will give you an unvarnished look at what it is like to own a franchise with their brand. No one understands the granular details of running that particular business better than them, and you will get pertinent details that will help you determine how potentially successful you will be if you choose to join the system.

Which Franchisees Do I Speak With?

As you begin validation, use these two criteria to decide which franchisees to speak with.

First, speak to those franchisees who live and operate their business in your area, if there are any. If it's a younger franchise brand and they don't have anyone else in your area, look for franchisees who live in the same kind of area you are in, from a demographic perspective. So, if you live in San Francisco, you should speak to franchisees who live in other large urban cities like New York and Washington D.C. If you live in Baltimore, M.D., you would want to speak with franchisees in other similar cities like Ann Arbor, M.I. or Alexandria, V.A. This will enable you to compare "apples to apples" in terms of determining how successful your business would be if you launched it in a similar market.

Second, speak to a cross-section of franchisees. In consultation with the franchise executive you are working with, pick franchisees who have been in business less than a year, some who have been in business for one to three years, and some who have been in business for more than five years. Not every single franchisee in any system will be a top performer. Remember the bell curve you studied in school? You will find that the distribution of franchisees within a franchise falls on the typical bell curve: the majority of franchisees will fall into the middle with a smaller percentage of top- and low-performing franchisees.

What Questions Should I Ask Them?

It was Tony Robbins who said, "Successful people ask better questions, and as a result, they get better answers." Asking the right questions during your franchise validation calls (and sometimes in-person meetings, if the franchisee is local and lives in your area) is critical. As you prepare for your conversations with franchisees, here are some of the key questions you should ask.

Understanding the Fit Between the Franchisee and the Franchise

1. What was your background before you became a franchisee?

With this question, you are trying to understand if there are any similarities in your background and theirs. You are also trying to understand what skills and strengths they brought with them into the business that made them successful or not.

Do you have the same or similar skill sets? If not, does the franchise allow hiring an employee who does have the skills?

2. Did you look at any other franchise before this one?

This will give you another level of insight into specific characteristics of the business model that makes it stand out from other franchises in the marketplace.

3. What made you decide to go with this brand?

Understanding what made a franchisee choose this brand over another will help you understand the strengths and competitive advantages of the brand. Ask what other brands they investigated. Are the businesses in the same industry or in a different one?

4. What are your responsibilities as the owner?

The day-to-day responsibilities of the franchisee shape their workday. Can you see yourself doing the same? Would you be happy doing the same? Do these tasks engage your strengths? Or would it be a stretch for you to take on these responsibilities? Think back to why you began investigating franchises in the first place. It was to be able to create the kind of life and lifestyle that you wanted. Will the day-to-day responsibilities of the owner allow you to do this?

5. What separates top performers from low performers in this system?

The answer to this question will give you yet more insights on if you have what it takes to succeed.

Understanding Franchise Support

1. What initial training did the franchise give you? How has the ongoing support been?

This is a great question to ask as you will be getting a view of how robust the training and support system of the franchise is. After they signed the Franchise Agreement and officially came on board as a franchisee, what did the corporate team help them with? How long was the training, and how effective was it? Were they assisted in locating real estate? Did they receive help to hire key people on the team?

After the initial period, in what ways did the franchise continue to support them? Were there visits to the location from the corporate team? Were there continuing education initiatives? Does the franchise hold an annual conference where all franchisees can come together to learn about the business and the industry, growth trends, opportunities, and challenges?

2. How was your launch?

What support did they get for their opening day? Was their opening successful? If there were challenges with their opening, you will want to dig deeper to understand why that happened.

3. **After you became a franchisee, were there unexpected or unforeseen challenges you faced? How did you handle it? How did the corporate team help?**

You can never be fully prepared for everything that will come your way when you are a business owner. So, when something unexpected happens, can you count on your franchise for support and guidance?

Understanding Earnings

1. **What were your expectations for annual revenue? How long did it take before you hit it?**

If you have found that the background and skills of the franchisee is a fit with yours, this specific question can give you great insight on how likely you will be in reaching your revenue expectations.

2. **How long were you in business before you broke even?**

The answer to this question will allow you to understand how much of a cash cushion to have on hand so you can continue to run the business until you break even.

3. **What was your annual net profit?**

Often referred to as the bottom line, understanding the net profit (subtracting expenses from revenues) gives you a clear picture of how quickly this particular business will help you achieve your financial goals.

4. Knowing what you know now, would you make the same decision to become a franchisee with this brand?

This is an excellent question because their answer reveals a lot about their overall experience. It may uncover some areas that are lacking within the franchise model, or it may simply show you that franchise ownership is not a good fit for this specific franchisee. A franchisee's overall happiness with their choice and their lifestyle is extremely important because this could be telling of what your happiness level would be as a business owner under this system. While you will generally be able to gauge their happiness by the other answers they provided, this specific question can yield more exact details.

Understanding Marketing

1. How does the franchise support you in your local marketing efforts?

Marketing is the lifeblood of a franchise. One of the key benefits of opening a franchise is that it is an already established and known brand. With an established brand comes marketing campaigns, collateral, systems, and best practices.

The franchisee's answer will help you understand how effective the franchisor's marketing campaigns are. It will also help you understand if they have had to create campaigns specific to their local market/ region and if that is something that the franchisor provides support on.

Find Your Tribe

As the singer Pharrell said, "collaborate with people you can learn from." The validation stage you are in now is extremely important because it gives you the wonderful opportunity to get honest perspective on how the business is run from someone who is doing it right now. This eliminates biases and "selling" language and simply allows for you to have an honest conversation and ask questions you may not want to ask the franchisor.

Additionally, if you do decide that this franchise model is the right one for you, these franchisees will become a part of your team and support system, so getting to know them prior to joining the franchise is beneficial! Before you validate with existing franchisees, make sure you know what questions to ask. The more questions you ask during validation, the more information you will have to make an educated decision. Buying a franchise is a big decision. Make sure you are gathering helpful feedback and information to help you make the final decision – go or no-go!

Congrats!

With validation done, you are getting close to the end of your due diligence process. You leaned in and dug deep. You asked hard questions and challenged your own assumptions about what you thought you knew. You went through enough materials and read enough business documents to get an MBA!

If you have really engaged in this process with the brands, you should now be at a point to be able to make a decision on whether to move forward with a brand or not.

When a client begins working with me, their first question invariably is: what franchise is right for me? The second most important question every client always asks is: once I find my franchise, how do I pay for it? In the next chapter, we will tackle this important issue.

8

Step 5 Continue Due Diligence – Fund Your Franchise

"The most important investment you can make is in yourself."
– Warren Buffett

In Chapter 7, you delved deep into the phase of your search known as "validation" where you spoke with franchisees of the various brands that your franchise coach introduced you to. Based on validation and the extensive due diligence that you have conducted over your search, you have found the franchise that is right for you and will help you achieve your goals! Congrats – your hard work has paid off in spades!

This is it. You are almost ready to start your franchise! Only one thing is left: finding the money you need to finance the franchise, franchise fees, inventory (if any), and working capital.

If you have googled franchise funding options, then you are likely feeling very overwhelmed right now! Where do you begin? How do you even know which funding option is right for you? How do you know that you are working with a reputable and ethical lender?

The Five Questions

There are many factors that will go into determining which financing option may be best for you. Here are the five key questions to consider as you embark on the funding process.

1. Which franchise are you starting?

There are more than 3,200 franchises in more than 100 categories and every single one of them has a different start-up cost. Each franchise that you investigate will vary significantly in terms of startup and operating costs, revenues, and profits. This will directly dictate how much money you will need to borrow.

2. What do you need to finance?

Depending on what franchise you are planning to buy, you may need to buy equipment, hire employees, lease commercial real estate, and more. What piece do you need funding for?

3. Are you buying a new franchise or one that already exists?

New franchises have more limited financing options than existing franchises. If you are already a franchisee with a location and are adding a second location or renovating the existing one, you will have more options for financing.

4. What is your credit score?

Simply put, the higher your score, the more financing options will be available to you. There are many resources out there today that allow you to check your score for free. Take advantage of them, and understand how your score determines what financing mechanisms may be available to you.

5. What personal assets do you have?

Do you have personal savings or retirement funds? These assets can make it easier for you to buy a franchise. If you are planning on getting an SBA loan, you will need a minimum of ten to twenty percent down payment.

As you begin to explore various financing options for your franchise, keep in mind that the International Franchise Association (IFA), the trade association for the franchise industry, has numerous programs and incentives for women, minorities, and veterans. There are also specialized programs offered by banks, credit unions, and state and local governments that you may be eligible to tap into.

Many clients, when they first begin working with me, have this notion that the more the franchise costs, the higher the returns they will get. This is simply not true. The cost of a franchise is not directly correlated to its returns. There are many factors that determine how much a franchise can make including industry category, the market in which the franchisee is operating, and the business model, among others. When you first begin the search process with your franchise coach, you may be tempted to lock yourself to businesses that fall into a particular investment range. Don't do that. Your franchise coach should ideally be able to show you a diverse set of brands at various price points that *all* have the potential return you are looking for.

When my clients begin their search process, I immediately introduce them to one of my trusted funding partners. My partners are professionals who understand the nuances and complexities of the franchise funding process. They intimately understand the franchise industry and how to best navigate it. They will work hand in hand with you to help you determine which particular funding option is best given your particular situation.

Here are the most common ways in which my clients have funded the franchise of their dreams.

Personal Savings

If you are investigating service or B2B franchises, many will be available for a lower initial investment than the typical retail or fixed-location franchise. If you can find a franchise that meets your income goals and needs for less than $100,000, then you may be able to fund the investment completely from available cash, thus avoiding the need for sourcing any additional funding.

SBA Loan

The SBA loan is a small business loan that is partially guaranteed by the government (the Small Business Administration). The standard SBA loan for franchisees is known as the 7(a). Because it is partly guaranteed against default by the government, it eliminates some of the risk for the financial institution who is issuing the loan.

This partial guarantee, which can cover up to eighty-five percent of a loan's amount, makes traditional lenders more willing to consider lending to small businesses which are often perceived as being "too risky."

Because SBA loans involve the government, the application process is known for being very thorough and restrictive. If you think you will apply for a SBA loan, you will need to prepare a lot of documentation and come armed with patience!

With some of the highest loan amounts, the longest repayment terms, and the lowest APR's available to small businesses, SBA loans may be one of your best financing options.

Veterans Express Loan

Veterans are historically some of the most successful owners of franchises because of the training and discipline they learned during their service. When you couple their drive and their ability to execute with franchising's unique capacity to train, support, and guide, you end up with a powerful combination.

The SBA's Express Loan for vets provides some of the best terms and interest rates.

Rollover for Business Startups (ROBS)

If you have a 401(k) or an individual retirement account (IRA), this may be one of the best financing options you have. A rollover for business startups (ROBS) allows you to invest retirement funds from your 401(k) or IRA into your business without paying early withdrawal penalties or taxes. Because this is not a loan, there is no debt to repay or interest payments to make.

A ROBS gives you access to your retirement funds to use in your business without having to borrow or cash it out. A ROBS 401(k) involves incorporating a new business and opening a new 401(k) under it. After setup is complete, you can transfer assets in from other retirement accounts and invest those funds directly in your new business. However, using a ROBS requires you to follow specific rules that govern how the account is set up, managed, and ultimately unwound.

Setting up a rollover for business startups (ROBS) requires you to create a C corporation (C-corp) and then establish a retirement plan like a 401(k) for that new C-corp. Then, you roll over funds from your existing personal 401(k) or IRA into the new company's retirement plan. Using the funds you have just rolled over, the new 401(k) plan purchases stock in the C-corp, at which point the ROBS 401(k) rollover is completed, and your startup is capitalized.

At least half of my clients use this method to fund their franchise. It remains one of the most popular ways to start a franchise. Because it is a specialized funding tool, however, you will want to engage the services of an expert who can guide you through the set-up and administer your account.

Franchise Financing

Some franchises will provide direct financing to their franchisees. This often takes the form of accepting a promissory note for part or all of the initial franchise fees owed. But it can also involve more extensive lending if the franchisor is financially strong enough to provide such a program. Not every brand offers in-house financing. Whether or not a franchise provides financing assistance is discussed in Item 10 (Financing) of the Franchise Disclosure Document. In your due diligence conversations with the franchise executive, be sure to ask if they have such financing plans in place for franchisees. As you compare any in-house financing with other loan options, you may indeed find that they offer better financial terms than banks making it more advantageous for you to go this route.

Friends and Family

In my experience, I have found that borrowing money from friends and family can turn out to be a huge landmine if you do not navigate it properly. Because a business, franchise or not, carries with it a certain amount of risk, you have to be careful about who and how much you ask for support.

A better alternative to asking for money is to outsource services to family and friends. For example, if you have an uncle who is an accountant, you can ask for his expertise which will save you some money. If you have a friend who is a lawyer, they can help in setting up your entity or provide their expertise in other ways. These are valuable services that you will inevitably need in setting up your franchise and is one way to keep your expenses down without outright asking for cash to support your franchise.

Bottom line: be very careful. Your friends and family make up your support system, and you don't want to do anything to jeopardize that.

Franchise Funding Organizations

I work with a number of the most reputable and established franchise funding organizations in the country. You can visit their websites to get a sense of the services they offer. All of them offer complimentary consultations to understand your situation better and to offer potential funding solutions.

1. Benetrends: www.benetrends.com
2. FranFund: www.franfund.com
3. Guidant: www.guidant.com

One of the benefits that my clients get from working with me is that I introduce them to the funding organization that I believe will be the best for them. This creates a seamless process for my clients in that they do not have to go through the additional angst of having to figure out which organization is reputable and what option will be best for them.

If you are working with a franchise coach, they should be able to do the same for you. This, again, is a big reason to work with a coach who already has an established network of funding relationships that she can readily refer you to.

As you go through your due diligence and search process, be sure to work closely with your accountant or CPA. If you don't have one, ask your franchise coach for recommendations. Especially when it comes to funding your business, options like the ROBS have certain tax implications. You want to work with a professional to ensure you are doing what is required and setting things up correctly along the way.

9

Step 6 – Conclude Due Diligence: Attend Discovery Day & Make a Decision

"As you start to walk on the way, the way appears."
– Rumi

Congrats! You have been on quite a journey.

Over the past several weeks and months, you have been speaking with franchise brands to get a deep dive into their business models. You have reviewed the business models and pored over the FDDs. From lead generation to marketing to operations, you have touched on every key aspect of the business to understand if it is the right fit for you. You then went on to validate with franchisees of all the brands, understanding from their perspective what it takes to run a successful business within that particular system. You have also been investigating the most optimal financing solutions to fund your franchise once you have found it.

As you weigh everything that you have learned, you are now at a point where you can make the determination of which business is your perfect fit. This can be a very exciting and nerve-wracking time! You are excited at having found the franchise that fits you! You are also nervous about making what will undoubtedly be a life-changing decision when you move forward with it! Feeling fear at this stage is very normal. As I say to all my clients, if someone said that they felt zero fear, I would be fearful for them! You are on the cusp of becoming an entrepreneur, owning and running your own business. This is a big deal!

Take a moment to celebrate how much you have learnt and how far you have come!

Discovery Day: What It Is

The last step in the process and arguably the most important stage before making the decision to proceed with owning and operating your own franchise is the Discovery Day. Discovery Day is a face-to-face meeting, usually at the corporate office of the franchise. It is called this because it used to be the way that prospective clients discovered who ran the franchise and learned about what it meant to be a franchisee with them. With the advent of technology, while you are able to research a lot about the brand on the internet, you are still unable to meet in-person with the executive team. This is one of the biggest benefits of Discovery Day as you will be meeting the people who, in essence, will become your work family for years to come. Meeting the executive team allows you to get a sense of who is running the company and setting the vision, how they support their franchisees, and the systems they have in place to support their success.

Discovery Day usually takes place at the franchisor's main headquarters or in some cases, at an actual franchised location that is usually in the same town/city of the franchisor's main office. Some discovery days are very structured and will have up to twenty candidates in attendance while others will be on a one-to-one basis.

At Discovery Day, you will have the opportunity to meet the franchisor's corporate staff, take a tour of the facility, tour one or more franchised location(s), meet existing franchisees, and test the products and services.

A Discovery Day visit should ideally serve to "seal the deal" for you, one way or the other. If you have liked everything that you have heard and seen through your due diligence process, Discovery Day becomes the way for you to confirm the educated decision that this is indeed the franchise that is right for you.

Discovery Day Best Practices

Given the critical importance of Discovery Day, it is key that you are prepared.

Here is a list of best practices based on hundreds of clients who attended Discovery Days before making their decision to move forward with their franchise.

- You will be researching several brands. Only accept invitations from the franchises that really interest you. Discovery Days are both time and money intensive. Don't attend if you already feel that the business may not be the right one for you.

- During validation, speak to as many franchisees as you can. When you are at Discovery Day, you can use this information to home in on what is most important to you or address any unanswered questions you may still have.

- Discovery Day is still very much part of the overall interview process. Up to this point, the franchise company has only spoken to you over the phone or, in some instances, spoken to you on a video call or webinar. This is the first opportunity for the franchise company to meet you in person. You have evaluated the franchises for fit. They, in turn, have done the same with you to understand if you will make a successful franchisee within their system. They will be paying close attention to how you behave in a group setting, how you interact one-on-one with others, etc.

- Dress professionally. First impressions are important. You want to come across as someone who cares about their professional appearance and took the time to "look good" for them.

- You will most likely be taken to lunch or dinner at some point in the program with executives from the franchise. Keep in mind that this is not a social engagement. Be personable and warm but professional. Be natural but don't let down your guard.

- They are taking note of the kinds of questions you ask. Your questions reveal your level of interest and due diligence you have already done. Serious questions indicate a serious candidate.

- During the due diligence process, every franchise you speak to will ask if your partner/spouse is on board and supportive of your desire to start a franchise. Even if you plan to run the franchise by yourself, franchises want to know that they are supportive. If you and you partner are seeing anything differently, you want to resolve these differences before you show up for Discovery Day. You want to present a united front to the franchise; otherwise you may end up getting eliminated from moving forward with them.

- Remember the franchises you have been speaking to have been monitoring you long before you were invited to Discovery Day. Every step of the way, they are trying to determine how responsive and cooperative you are. Can you follow directions in a timely manner? Did you complete the tasks you were assigned as you moved through the due diligence process with them? Did you do it timely, or did they need to keep following up with you? If you cannot complete simple tasks in a timely fashion, how are you going to run a business?

- Discovery Days overflow with information, and franchise executives are taking note of your demeanor. They are watching how you engage not just with their team but with your fellow candidates who are also attending the event. How are you treating administrative staff at their office and wait staff at the restaurant? Are you friendly but authoritative? Or are you rude and aggressive?
- As you interact with the franchise executives, determine whether you will fit into their system and culture.
- As you interact with the other candidates who are attending Discovery Day, ask yourself if you are like them.
- Be on your best behavior, and bring your A game!

Discovery Day Checklist

____ Get directions to the location

____ Reserve hotel room (if necessary)

____ Reserve transportation to Franchise's corporate headquarters (if necessary)

____ Find out what portion of expenses are paid by the franchise. Some brands will cover all or part of the expenses for travel and accommodation.

_____ Remember to save receipts for reimbursement or taxable expenses

_____ Bring list of questions that have not yet been answered

_____ Find out what the appropriate dress is for the franchise's Discovery Day (It is typically business casual)

_____ Certified check – Ask the franchise what their initial deposit fee or franchise fee is

_____ All disclosures should be signed and returned to the franchise with the appropriate waiting periods met

_____ All decision makers should attend Discovery Day

_____ Verify all registration forms have been sent to the franchise (if applicable)

After Discovery Day, you will be contacted by the franchise with one of two responses. The franchise may tell you that the executive team, based on their interactions with you, did not feel that you would be a good fit with their system. While this can be very disappointing, you should take this as positive feedback. If you get this response, thank them professionally for their time and move on. They know more about their brand and culture than you do. You don't want to be a part of a family in which you will be a misfit. You can now cross this franchise off your list and focus on other options that are a better fit for you and your goals. Understanding what businesses are not a fit with you takes you one step closer to finding the business that is.

Many clients think that if they have enough money they can buy a franchise. That simply is not the case. Franchises are awarded, not bought. Franchisors will make the decision to award you a franchise if they feel that the fit is there, and both parties will be successful and happy together for years to come.

The response that you will be waiting for obviously is the one where the franchisor informs you that they have made the decision to award you a franchise if you would like to move forward with them. Congratulations! This is a big deal. Understand that you are a small percentage of prospective franchisees who make it successfully through the due diligence process to be awarded a franchise. You did your part, and you are now being invited to join the family of a reputable franchise brand.

At this stage in the process, the franchise will send you the Franchise Agreement for your review and signature. At this point, I typically tell my clients, "Time out." They are excited and ready to move forward with the franchise. I tell them that there is one last thing they should consider doing before signing the agreement. I recommend that they have the agreement be reviewed by a reputable franchise attorney. I work with some of the best in the country and refer my clients to them. Of course, this is a completely personal decision and one that you can either choose to do or not. Almost all of my clients will have their agreement reviewed by an attorney to fully understand their rights, roles, and responsibilities in the franchise/franchisee relationship.

In my experience, here are the three key reasons to hire a franchise attorney.

1. Industry expertise

Remember the 200+ plus page FDD that you reviewed, cover to cover? There are certain restrictions, obligations, and responsibilities you will have as a franchisee, and you could be terminated if you don't abide by them. Your franchise attorney will help you understand these. You will want to work with a franchise attorney who has also written a few FDDs themselves so they know exactly what to look for when they are reviewing yours. They also stay up to date on franchise laws which change all the time.

A reputable and knowledgeable franchise attorney will be a valuable resource for you now and for years to come.

2. Business entity guidance

A reputable franchise attorney can offer useful suggestions on how your new franchise business should be set up. Should your business be a Limited Liability Corporation (LLC)? A Subchapter S Corporation? C-Corporation? Do you know the differences?

Choosing the right business entity for your new franchise is crucial. It will determine your legal rights and liabilities as a business owner. It will also determine how your business is taxed. So, get it set up right from the get-go.

3. If you fail...

You are not starting a franchise expecting that it will fail. However, that is still a possibility. In the event that something goes south with you and your franchise, you always want to be able to say that you got your FDD and Franchise Agreement reviewed by a franchise attorney who made you aware of your rights and responsibilities as a franchisee.

Once you have done the review and are satisfied with the feedback from your attorney, you are now ready to move forward. You will sign the agreement and pay the franchise fee, either with a wire transfer or certified check. You have now officially become a franchisee!

The Path Unfolds When You Begin

Every week, I speak with would-be entrepreneurs. They wax eloquently about why they want to start a business. Then, almost immediately, they start listing reasons (or excuses, to be clear) why they cannot. There is not enough time to do the research to find the right business. With their background, what franchise would be a fit anyway? Their spouse wants them to get a job. What if they fail? Can the franchise ensure their success?

Notice something about all these excuses? They begin with the presumption of failure. They also show up when someone does not fully accept responsibility for the outcomes in their life. As with anything else in life, what you do consistently will determine your results.

Entrepreneurship is not easy. Otherwise everyone would be doing it. It is, however, incredibly rewarding because it truly shows you what you are made of. Most people will choose to live their lives in quiet desperation, working at jobs that they hate because they are too scared to carve a new path forward. Few will work past those very same fears to chart a map through the unknown territory of business ownership. You are now a part of those few.

You belong to the small minority of people who took the path less traveled. As you started to explore franchise ownership, you trusted the process. You gave up the need to know everything. You let your curiosity lead you. You overcame your fears by focusing on the possibility of a better life for you and your family. And, once you began, the path unfolded.

10

Your Franchise Coach

"A coach is someone who tells you what you don't want to hear and has you see what you don't want to see, so you can be who you have always known you can be."

– Tom Landry

You now know what your franchise search process looks like. You understand the various steps of the process and what they entail. Before you embark on your search, there is one key thing which can spell the difference between success and failure in finding your perfect fit franchise: working with a franchise coach.

While you can certainly conduct a franchise search on your own, know that you will almost certainly encounter false starts, review franchises that "look good" on the surface but fall apart upon closer analysis, and spend a lot of time spinning your wheels. The franchise industry is incredibly complex and nuanced. Engage a professional who understands this industry and let them help you navigate through the maze of potential franchise opportunities.

As you consider researching franchises, I hope you make the decision to work with a franchise coach. This is the key to a successful search that ends in you finding the perfect fit franchise of your dreams. I have had numerous clients who found me after they had gone it alone and ended up spinning their wheels and wasting time and energy. I have also had clients who came to me after losing their investment in a franchise that they had found on their own.

What Exactly is a Franchise Coach?

As the name suggests, a franchise coach is a franchise industry expert. She assists you in understanding your personal goals from a franchise, and then introduces you to a handful of franchises that may be the perfect fit for you. From franchise selection to helping you evaluate the various aspects of the different business models, she works one-on-one with you to get clear on whether a particular franchise will meet your goals. Because she understands the nuances of the franchise industry, your franchise coach can help you navigate potential landmines. She acts as your coach, helping you course-correct along the way, if needed. In addition to helping you home in on your perfect fit franchise, your coach will also work with you to suggest the best resources and funding options to access the capital you need to own and operate your franchise.

If she is reputable and knows her craft, your franchise coach will become your one-stop shop for all things franchise.

If you own your own home, think back to when you were looking for it. What was the first thing you did? You probably spoke to family and friends or looked online for a buyer's real estate broker that you could work with. Why did you do that? Could you have looked for houses on your own? Why didn't you?

A real estate agent acts as the intermediary between her client (the buyer) and the person who is selling their home (the seller). After a consultation with you, your agent got a better understanding of what you were looking for in a house. They also found out how much you could afford. In other words, they pre-qualified or pre-approved you for a certain amount. Armed with key information on you, they then presented various options that met your criteria (e.g., this house has four bedrooms, three baths, all hardwood floors, a large deck overlooking the woods, and an in-law suite in the basement).

What Does Your Franchise Coach Do?

She goes through a detailed consultation with you during which she gets a better understanding of why you are looking to buy a franchise and what you want from the franchise, your goals (e.g., I am looking for a franchise that allows me to work on my schedule, with no employees, where I don't have to invest any more than $150,000, and be able to replicate a six-figure income). Armed with this and other key information, your franchise coach then presents you with franchise options that meet these criteria.

Throughout the search process, your franchise coach provides you with objective information that the franchise will not. In addition to introducing you to the best financing options for your franchise, she will also introduce you to franchise attorneys who will provide another set of impartial eyes to your franchise agreement before you sign it and commit to the franchise.

Where Do You Find Your Franchise Coach?

In today's professional world, LinkedIn has become the preeminent networking platform for all things career-related. You can do a search for "franchise coach" or "franchise consultant." There are hundreds of professionals who list this as their profession. As with anything else, no two coaches are the same. You have to do your due diligence to find someone who will be the best resource for *you*. This can be tricky.

So, how do you find a coach who is right for you? Who can you work with who will guide you not only in your search for the "perfect fit" franchise but even beyond? In my experience working with hundreds of clients and the feedback I have received from them, there are three key characteristics of a great franchise coach.

"Everyone needs a coach, whether it's a top-level executive, a graduate student, a homemaker, a homeless person, or the President of the United States." Tony Robbins, arguably the world's foremost personal development coach, said. A great franchise coach will help you do three key things as you embark upon and go through your franchise search process.

She will work with you to:

1. Get clear on your goals from a franchise

Before your coach presents you with any franchise options, she will want to spend time with you getting to know who you are and to really understand *you*. What do I mean?

With every client of mine, I typically spend anywhere from two to four hours with each of them *before* I make even a single franchise recommendation. I have found that the franchise search process is essentially an iterative endeavor. It is critical for me to get a better understanding of who my client is beyond her resume and LinkedIn profile. Most of my clients laugh when I ask them: "Who is the real Mary? What are those things that when you are doing them make your eyes sparkle and your heart sing? What are those things that you do better than anyone else you know? These are your superpowers. Conversely, what are those things that you would rather get your healthy tooth pulled out without lidocaine than do?! These are your blind spots and weaknesses." I get to know my clients intimately. I understand who they are and what makes them tick. I uncover their deeper motivations for entrepreneurship, their hidden desires for something more. Your franchise coach should get to know you and understand you this well.

When You Are Clear ... Your Life Will Take Off.

A retired police officer, Andrew came to me and expressed an interest in buying a food/burger concept. Upon asking him why, he said that he loved the idea of owning a restaurant and recounted his own experiences as a customer at various burger joints. This is exactly the wrong reason to want to become a business owner! The experience of being a customer is completely different from the experience of owning the establishment that a customer is in. As a business owner, you are responsible for all manners of things that a customer simply does not have to think about. In addition, Andrew was completely misinformed about the investment amount needed to open a location of this particular burger franchise. As I spent time with him uncovering what he wanted from a business and how much money he had and wanted to invest, it became very clear to him that a food franchise was the last thing he wanted to start. Over the next few months, I worked with Andrew to find him a home services franchise that fit his skillset and his investment level. Additionally, this franchise cost him less than one-fifth of what it would have taken him to start the burger joint but had the potential for a higher return on his investment (ROI)!

Andrew's motivation for starting a business stemmed from his previous career as a first responder. As a police officer, he was the bridge between his local community and law enforcement. As an entrepreneur, he wanted to start a business that provided a service to his customers while building wealth for his future. Had I not spent time uncovering

Andrew's goals and needs from a franchise, I would not have been able to pinpoint the franchise that he went on to start.

Make sure you are working with a franchise coach who first understands your needs before she makes any recommendations. First and foremost, your coach should get a deep and detailed sense of who you are and what you bring to the table. There are thousands of franchise options out there, but there is only one you. Which one franchise stands out from the rest in being able to match your skills and meet your needs?

2. Move past your fears

Maya Angelou once said, "Hope and fear cannot occupy the same space. Invite one to stay."

If only it were that easy. Hope and fear are actually two sides of the same coin. If you have ever started a new job, had a new baby, decided to get married, gotten a driver's license, or had a new experience, you have probably felt fear. It is a universal emotion. The good news is that fear is not always a bad thing. In fact, it can be a great thing – as long as it is channeled the right way.

You are reading this book because you are contemplating buying into a franchise. If the fear you feel is a red flag that prevents you from jumping headfirst into a venture without doing your due diligence, then this fear is good and empowering. It cautions you to minimize your risk and protects you from rash decisions that will negatively impact your life.

On the other hand, fear can also be a debilitating feeling that stops you in your tracks before you've even given yourself the chance to explore something new. Sometimes, a new opportunity can be the chance of a lifetime. This kind of fear is self-destructive and disempowering. It leads us to hold on to situations that are not good for us – like staying in a toxic work environment because the fear of the unknown is too overwhelming.

Which kind of fear would you rather have? The empowering fear that acts to protect you and help you make good decisions? Or the disempowering fear that creates drag in your career and life and keeps you locked in destructive disabling situations?

Does the thought of starting a franchise, breaking with your career, charting an unknown path scare you? Good! It simply means you are human. As fear rises, take a deep belly breath and go inwards. Ask yourself: Why? What about this scares me? Am I acting too quickly? Do I know too little about what I am getting into? Am I scared of failing? Am I scared of being successful? What will success mean? Am I scared because I might lose friends and family?"

Helping clients manage their fears – and harness them to their advantage – is a key part of the work I do with my clients as their franchise coach. The coach you work with should do the same for you.

Fear Makes The Wolf Bigger Than He Is

When Peggy came to me, she had been a stay-at-home mom to two preteens for several years. When she and her husband moved to the United States from Latin America, they had made the decision for her to take care of the children. Her husband traveled constantly for his work and was almost never around, making it even more imperative for her to take on the role of primary caretaker.

Before she moved to the U.S., Peggy was the Director of Human Resources at one of the top accounting firms in the world. She had led large teams of people, managed strategic initiatives, and led growth for her company. When she began working with me, she had gotten deeply frustrated by the lack of corporate opportunities that fit where she was in her life. She had started wondering if a franchise was the best option for her and her family. Over the course of the next couple of months, I worked with her to evaluate various franchise brands. She had a lot of fears around losing the investment, not being able to grow the business, and not being able to be successful as an entrepreneur. Many of her fears were not rooted in reality. She began to understand that most of her fears were addressed and eliminated by doing thorough due diligence to understand the business inside and out.

Peggy is now the successful owner of a franchise that provides staffing services to mid- and large-sized companies. And those fears that reared their ugly heads? They are nowhere to be seen!

My advice? Welcome the good fear. Rational fear can propel you to do thorough research, ask better questions, and make informed decisions. So who knows? Maybe fear and hope can occupy the same space.

3. Set you up for success *after* you have become a franchisee

Once my clients sign on the dotted lines of their franchise agreement, the adventure starts! They are embarking on a new life as an entrepreneur. They are filled with hope and trepidation and have a million questions! My work with my clients does not end when they sign on the dotted lines. I continue to work with them, albeit in an informal capacity, to act as a resource and trusted advisor. I have introduced former clients to local CPAs in their markets, franchise attorneys to guide them through the formation of their new business, commercial insurance agents and real estate brokers to secure their locations, among many others.

A great coach intuitively understands that a transactional relationship with a client on the front end yields transactional results on the back end. She should be a resource for you for years to come as you grow and scale your franchise.

Do I Have to Work with a Franchise Coach?

I have had many people who attend my franchise workshops ask me if they should work with someone like me. My answer, quite simply, is this: *yes!* You have nothing to lose and a whole lot to gain!

The services of a franchise coach are offered at no cost to you. Further, if after working with a coach you determine that a franchise is not the right option for you, you are under no obligation to invest. So, do you end up paying more for your franchise if you work with a coach versus another potential candidate who finds the same franchise on their own? The answer is no. Franchises cannot charge one franchisee one fee and another franchisee a different amount. That would quite simply be illegal.

Your franchise coach is a free – and valuable – resource for you. Let your coach go to work for you. It may be the best investment in expertise you ever made!

11

Dare to Live the Life You Have Always Wanted!

"She, In the dark,
Found light, brighter than many ever see.
She, Within herself,
Found loveliness, Through the soul's own mastery.
And now the world receives, From her dower:
The message of the strength, Of inner power."
– Langston Hughes

By reading this book, you have taken the first step towards your decision to start a franchise business.

My hope for you is that you will use this proven six-step process to help you find your perfect fit franchise – the franchise that fits you and your life!

So, let's recap each step of your search process and the key takeaways from each.

The search process consists of six steps, done in sequential order.

Step 1: Conduct Your Personal Franchise Analysis

In this step, you took an introspective inventory of *you!* You began listing your strengths and weaknesses, your likes and dislikes. You reflected back on your career to times when you felt "in flow." What were you doing? Conversely, you thought back to times when the task at hand felt like an uphill battle every step of the way? What were you doing then?

Uncovering these aspects of yourself is key *before* you begin to search for a franchise that is the right fit for you. Different franchises require different strengths, and you need to understand how your skill set aligns with a specific franchise model.

A great franchise coach will be able to guide you through this critical first step of the process.

Step 2: Build Your Franchise Business Model

Your business model is a picture of your perfect franchise. It includes all the characteristics of a business that you are looking for that are important to you. In consultation with you, your franchise coach will build your business model. This then becomes the blueprint or roadmap that you will use for your search.

There are more than 3,200 franchises in the United States alone. Some are home-based, while others are brick-and-mortar businesses. Some require hands-on management, while others semi-absentee ownership. Some require owners who are skilled at sales and networking; others are looking for franchisees who are operational gurus. Every franchise, just like you, is unique.

Using the personal assessment that you completed in Step 1, you will incorporate your skill sets into your business model. Your franchise coach will then begin the process of matching franchises whose business models most closely match your business model. You will now start to evaluate franchises that are a fit versus those that may not be.

Step 3: Begin Due Diligence – Speak with Franchises

Armed with your personal assessment and your business model, you are now ready to begin the process referred to in the franchise industry as due diligence.

At the start of due diligence, your franchise coach introduces you to a number of franchises that she selected based on your business model. These are franchises that may be a fit based on the personal, financial, and lifestyle goals that you shared with your coach and identified as important to you.

Each franchise will go through and review the major components of their business model with you. Key aspects of a business model may include lead generation, local marketing, operations, hiring employees, business development, etc. You will have weekly calls with the franchises as well as webinars and videos.

Each business will also share their Franchise Disclosure Document (FDD) with you. This legal document is comprised of twenty-three items or sections which give you a comprehensive overview of the financial state of the franchise, including any outstanding litigation against them and earnings claims of existing franchisees.

The objective of this step is for you to uncover how a particular franchise operates, and in doing so, you are trying to understand if this is a franchise that *you* can operate successfully based on the skills you bring to the table.

Step 4: Continue Due Diligence – Speak with Franchisees

As you move through the due diligence process, you will enter into the phase known as validation. During validation, each franchise will introduce you to a number of current franchisees in their system with whom you will validate everything that the franchise has shared with you until now, including the earnings claims in the FDD.

While, you now have a detailed idea of how a franchise operates, you are still unclear on what the day-to-day operations of a franchisee looks like. During validation, you speak with franchisees of the brands you are investigating to get a granular feel for what it is really like to run a particular business. Through your conversations with franchisees, you will ask questions that are most important to you to understand what running the business is like.

This is possibly the most invaluable part of your research.

Step 5: Continue Due Diligence – Fund Your Franchise

As soon as you begin investigating franchise options, your franchise coach will concurrently set you up with a franchise funding partner to begin the process of figuring out how to fund your franchise, once you've found it. There are numerous options, some that may be suitable for you and others that may not, based on an analysis of your specific financial situation.

Knowing how much you can comfortably afford and how you will fund the business will take a big load off your mind, freeing you to focus completely on your search.

Step 6: Conclude Due Diligence – Attend Discovery Day & Make a Decision

You are now almost at the end of your due diligence. There are two key things to focus on at this stage.

As you end the validation phase, you will be invited (if the franchise feels that there is a great fit with you!), to what is known as a Discovery Day. A discovery day is an opportunity for you to visit the franchise's corporate headquarters. Franchises use this as a way to interview the potential candidate (you) in person and see if there is a mutual fit. You should also take this as an opportunity to learn more about the company and the operations team. They will become your extended work family for years to come.

After Discovery Day, if you like the franchise and they like you, the franchise will formally invite you to become a part of their franchisee family. Remember that a franchise is awarded to you once the brand feels that there is a fit between who they are and what you bring to the table. The franchise will present you with the Franchise Agreement, which is the legal binding contract that lays out the responsibilities of each party – the franchisor, the franchise company, and you, the franchisee.

If you have done your research diligently and have attended Discovery Day, you are in a position to make your decision. Either you want to move forward into ownership, or you know why you don't. Check in with yourself. The decision to move forward must sit comfortably on an emotional, business, and financial level. With the help of your franchise coach, you have now found your perfect fit franchise!

Once you have your agreement in hand, your franchise coach will refer you to a reputable franchise attorney to get it reviewed. Before you begin this new relationship with your franchise, you will want to be clear about your roles, responsibilities, and obligations as a franchisee to maximize your chances of success.

Sophia Revisited

Let's take a moment to revisit Sophia who you met in the first chapter of the book.

Like you, Sophia had gotten to a point where she felt that she was out of sync with her career and her life. Her career no longer fit her. Her life did not feel like hers. It was as though life was passing her by. As the years passed, she continued to feel more and more conflicted about the numerous family sacrifices she had made for her job. She hungered for something more, something different.

Sophia's breakthrough moment came when her best friend got laid off from the company that they both worked at. The more she thought about it, she realized that she could no longer afford to maintain the status quo and continue each day as though nothing was wrong. In a moment of brutal honesty, she realized that she, like other colleagues before her, was only a number on the company's balance sheet. She was in very real danger of getting laid off herself, anytime.

Once she made the decision to change her career trajectory, she began to explore franchises as a viable option for herself and her family. Sophia began working with me. While she did not know very much at all about franchises, she had read and seen enough to know that many people had found success through it. At this point in her life, she was ready to redefine success on her own terms. She wanted a business that she would be the boss of. She wanted to do work that she would be proud of, on a schedule of her choosing. This would enable her to spend more time with her two young daughters in a way that she had never before been able to. She also understood that her financial upside would only be limited by her desire to grow and succeed!

Three months later, Sophia became the proud owner of a franchise that provides leadership training to managers at small and mid-sized companies. She had found a business that required the formidable skills that she had honed over the years as a corporate executive. The same skills that had made her successful in her corporate career were the very same ones that she would need to use to grow and scale her new business. By operating in her zone of genius, she was confident that she would be able to grow a very successful business. She built a new work life around her family and their needs, not the other way around! She created a work schedule that allowed her to focus fully on building her new business while her daughters were at school. She "closed down" once she picked them up. Her new life brought her a sense of peace and purpose – two key attributes that were missing when she was a corporate executive.

As with other clients I have placed in franchises, Sophia soon realized that a franchise that fits you does not just help you create a *career* you love; it helps you create a *life* you love! Being able to spend more time with her two daughters and her husband has given Sophia a level of personal fulfillment that she had never imagined before.

When I met Sophia again almost a year after I had placed her in her business, I felt like I was meeting a completely different woman. She had a glow about her. She was happy, contented. I could sense it in her energy and her body language. She wakes up each morning without an alarm. She is grateful to have another day to do work that she loves! As she sits at her kitchen table sipping her oolong tea, she says that the red cardinal that she first noticed when her best friend got laid off, no longer came to sit on the old oak tree in her backyard. In a weird way, she feels that the little bird was a good omen come to signal that she needed to change the trajectory of her life. Once she left the corporate world to start her business, she said that the bird no longer appeared.

Its work was done. She looked at me and teared up, a gentle smile on her face.

So, Where Are *You* Headed?

When you are no longer what you were but have not yet become who you are meant to be, between the two lie a space pregnant with amazing possibilities! If you feel that your life no longer fits who you have become, pay attention to it.

Ask: why?

Ask: what can I do about it?

I wrote this book to share the six-step successful and proven process that I have used with countless clients to help them find the franchise that is right for them. Every client was unique. They had different life stories and challenges, superpowers and blind spots. Yet, each had essentially the same desire: the desire to create a better, more fulfilled, more financially rewarding career and life. And they all felt that a franchise was the vehicle that would help them achieve their goals.

As a former corporate executive myself, I can tell you that the life I now live is so very different and so much better than anything I could have ever imagined. As professionals, we talk about the elusive work-life balance. It is the mythical unicorn that no one has ever seen. When I was in career transition, I knew that whatever I did next would have to bring me both peace and purpose. Without work-life balance, we become shells of ourselves continuously and relentlessly grinding away in the pursuit of an objective that perhaps never was ours to begin with. Over time, not only do we become less productive in our work, we lose touch with our own essence.

Did you identify with any of the clients whose stories I have shared throughout the book? Did you read about some part of their journey and said to yourself: "That sounds just like me!" If you see your own life story in theirs, you owe it to yourself to explore the potential of a franchise. If you see your own struggles in the stories of Sophia, Colin, Anne, Nate, or any of my other clients in this book- know that you are not alone.

A franchise, like anything else in life, is not for everyone. It is, however, the option of choice for thousands. Make the decision now to explore if this option could be right for you too.

Wrest control of your life back from your employer for you are the master of your fate and the captain of your soul.

Who knows you may finally be able to escape the nine-to-five, generate true wealth, and finally live life on your own terms!

ACKNOWLEDGMENTS

For years, people had told me to write a book. For years, I laughed it off publicly and then wondered privately if I could. Finally one day, for no rhyme or reason, I knew it was time. Writing a book is harder than I had ever thought it would be when I started. It is also more rewarding than I could have ever imagined. Writing is a lonely process, at times, and this book would not have been possible without the love and support of these amazing individuals.

My parents, Kamal & Neela: without the two of you, this book would never have been born. You taught me the value of hard work, integrity, manners and grace. From the day I was born, you showed me through your own lives that absolutely anything is possible. Over the years, you were the wind that lifted my wings. This book is for you.

My husband, Peter: You are my oxygen. Your unfailing support and enthusiasm for everything I do makes you my biggest cheerleader. I love you so much.

My daughter, Zeryn: your shining spirit is a reminder every day of what it is like to live a life bursting at the seams with joy and authenticity! I love you more than any words I can write.

My sister, Monjuri: you've been beside me in every major (and minor) life event. You have been my companion through the peaks and the valleys. Our polar opposite traits, combined together, do indeed make us the real wonder woman!

My brother-in-law, Murshed: you expertly helped me navigate my myriad dental adventures while this book was being written so I wouldn't go mental! You are a dentist extraordinaire and one of the nicest guys around! My sister is lucky to have you… or is it the other way around?

My dear friends: Our circle is small but tight. You've known me for years and stood by me through my struggles and cheered on all my successes. That is true friendship.

My book support team, Cheyenne Giesecki and Ramses Rodriguez: Writing a book about my life and career is… strange. So many times, it felt like an out-of-body experience, and you were always there to pull me back into my body! Mere words cannot express my gratitude to you.

My editors: Mehrina Asif and Moriah Howell, you lovely ladies took the gibberish I handed to you and helped me make sense of it! Your editorial help and keen insights helped bring my stories to life. It is because of your honest feedback and endless encouragement that I have a legacy to pass on to my family where one did not exist before.

David Hancock and the Morgan James Publishing team: a heartfelt thanks for helping me bring this book to print!

Angela Lauria: you are the teacher I did not know I was searching for. I continue to learn from your remarkable courage and integrity, every day.

Tory Burch: you showed me what is possible. Working with you was a privilege and a dream come true. To this day, I "embrace ambition" as my right.

Will Rosenzweig: my dear gardener, your quiet wisdom fills my heart and replenishes it when it grows weary. Your guidance over the years has helped me understand what it means to become "businessworthy". I am deeply grateful that you saw something in me and encouraged me to create a path where none existed.

Nick Neonakis: where do I even begin, my dear friend? When there was no way forward, you gave me a map to chart the path ahead. You then carried the lamp that lit the way.

My clients: I get to live my calling every day because of you. Thank you for placing your trust in me. It is the privilege of my life to be able to work with you and learn from you.

My franchise partners: I am awed when I think about the companies that you have built and that you represent. These are household brands that have helped transform the lives of thousands of franchisees and their families. I am grateful to be able to work with you and help you find your perfect fit franchisee!

THANK YOU!

Thank you for reading this book!

In a sea of millions of books, you picked this one up for a reason. Perhaps the title spoke to you? Perhaps you sensed it contained the message you needed just when you needed it. Whatever the reason, I hope you found the material of value.

If you are searching for an alternative career option that does not involve the corporate world and think that business ownership may be for you, let's explore together!

Email me at Faizun@FaizunKamal.com if you would like to set up a complimentary consultation to begin the conversation.

With gratitude,
Faizun

Connect with Me!

On LinkedIn:

https://www.linkedin.com/in/faizunkamal/

On Twitter:

https://twitter.com/faizun_kamal

On Facebook:

https://www.facebook.com faizunkamalFRANCHISE/

By email:

Faizun@FaizunKamal.com

"Stop Making A Living; Start Designing A Life!"

— Faizun Kamal

ABOUT THE AUTHOR

Faizun Kamal is the CEO of the franchise consulting firm, The Franchise Pros, and the best-selling author of *The Right Franchise for You: Escape the 9 to 5, Generate Wealth, & Live Life on Your Terms.*

As CEO of The Franchise Pros, Faizun coaches people nationwide on making the transition from employee to entrepreneur. A corporate refugee herself, she has helped countless executives find their "perfect fit" franchise based on an assessment of their personal, professional, lifestyle, and income goals. As a nationally renowned public speaker, she inspires professionals to proactively move beyond career burnout to build a sustainable career and, in turn, a life that they love!

Faizun's drive to make a difference stems from her own personal experience as a corporate refugee. In 2015, after almost a decade in the corporate world, she was laid off. Instead of immediately jumping back into another job, Faizun began a deeply introspective journey to intentionally redesign her career and her life. Through the world of franchising, she discovered a way to live a life of purpose, passion, and profit!

Her experiences as a former Fortune 15 Executive with more than eighteen years of experience in corporate, multinational, nonprofit, and entrepreneurial settings on three continents have made her an inspirational speaker to audiences worldwide. Faizun's relatability and authenticity has led her to grow an engaged following of thousands on social media.

The Tory Burch Foundation named Faizun as "A Woman to Watch." She has been featured extensively on *Forbes, The Huffington Post,* and *The Washington Business Journal,* among many others. Faizun received her BA in Women's Studies and Environmental Studies from Mount Holyoke College. She holds a Master's degree in Public Policy and a Master's in Business Administration from the Johns Hopkins University. She is also a graduate of Stanford University's acclaimed Social Entrepreneurship Program.

She lives with her family in Alexandria, Virginia.

9 781642 798685